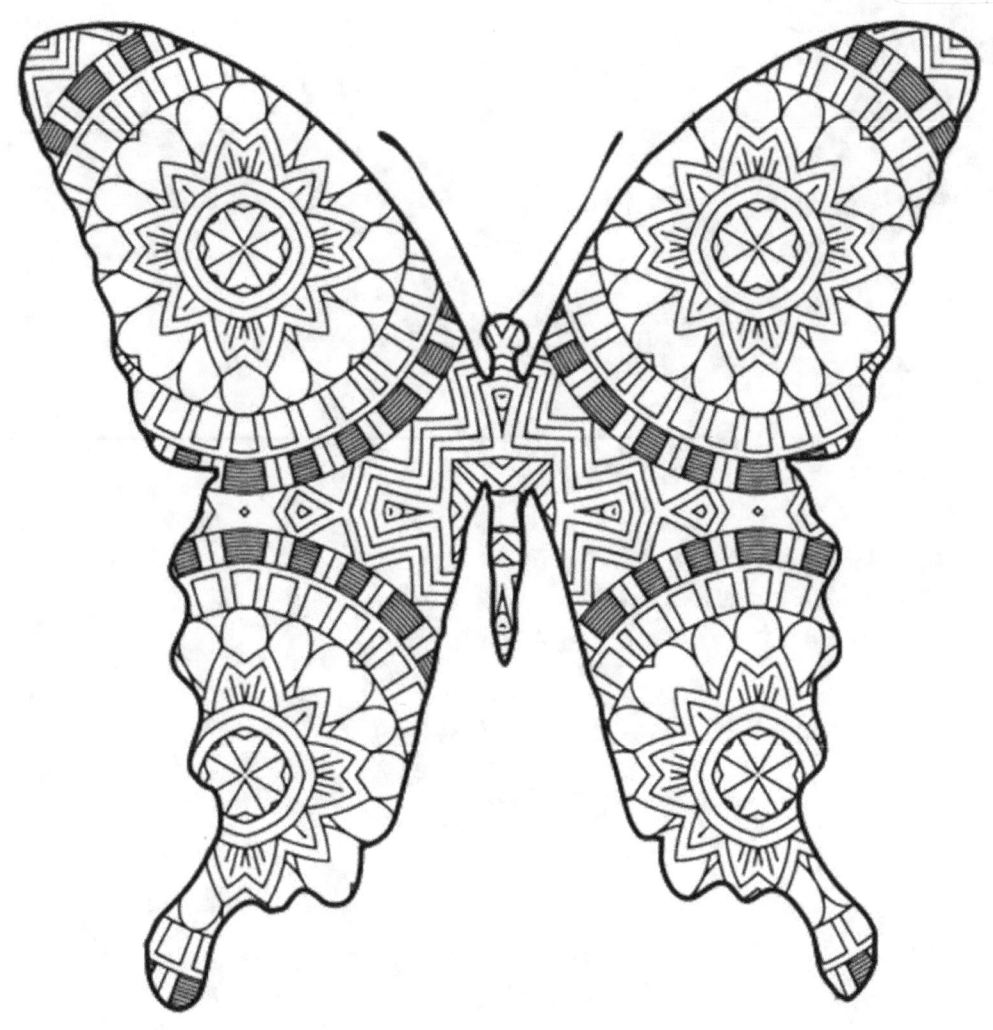

This book belongs to:

_____

_____

_____

_____

All rights reserved. May not be replicated or reproduced, in any form or by any means, without written permission from the publisher.

Copyright © 2020 by KT Designs Books

Color Test Page

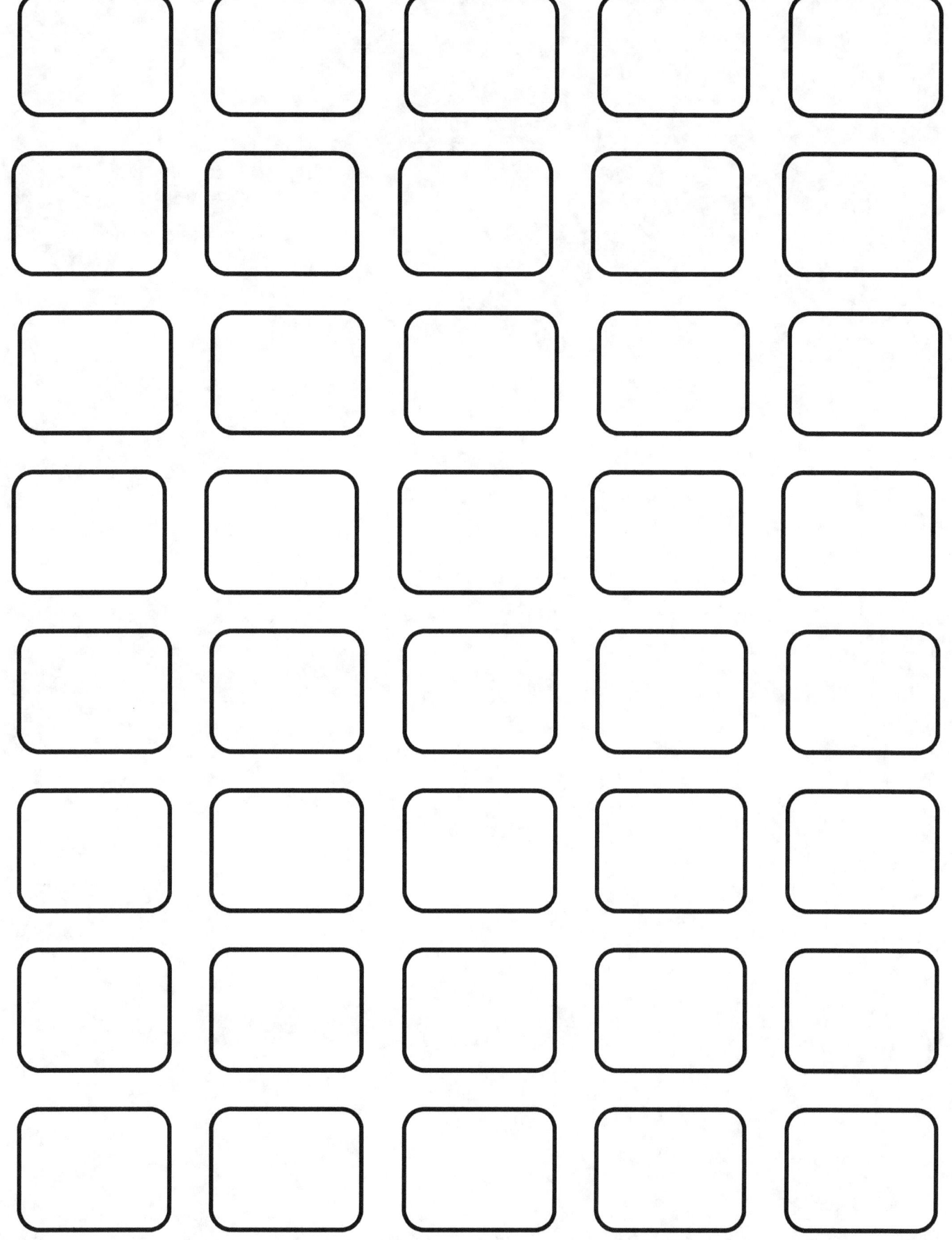

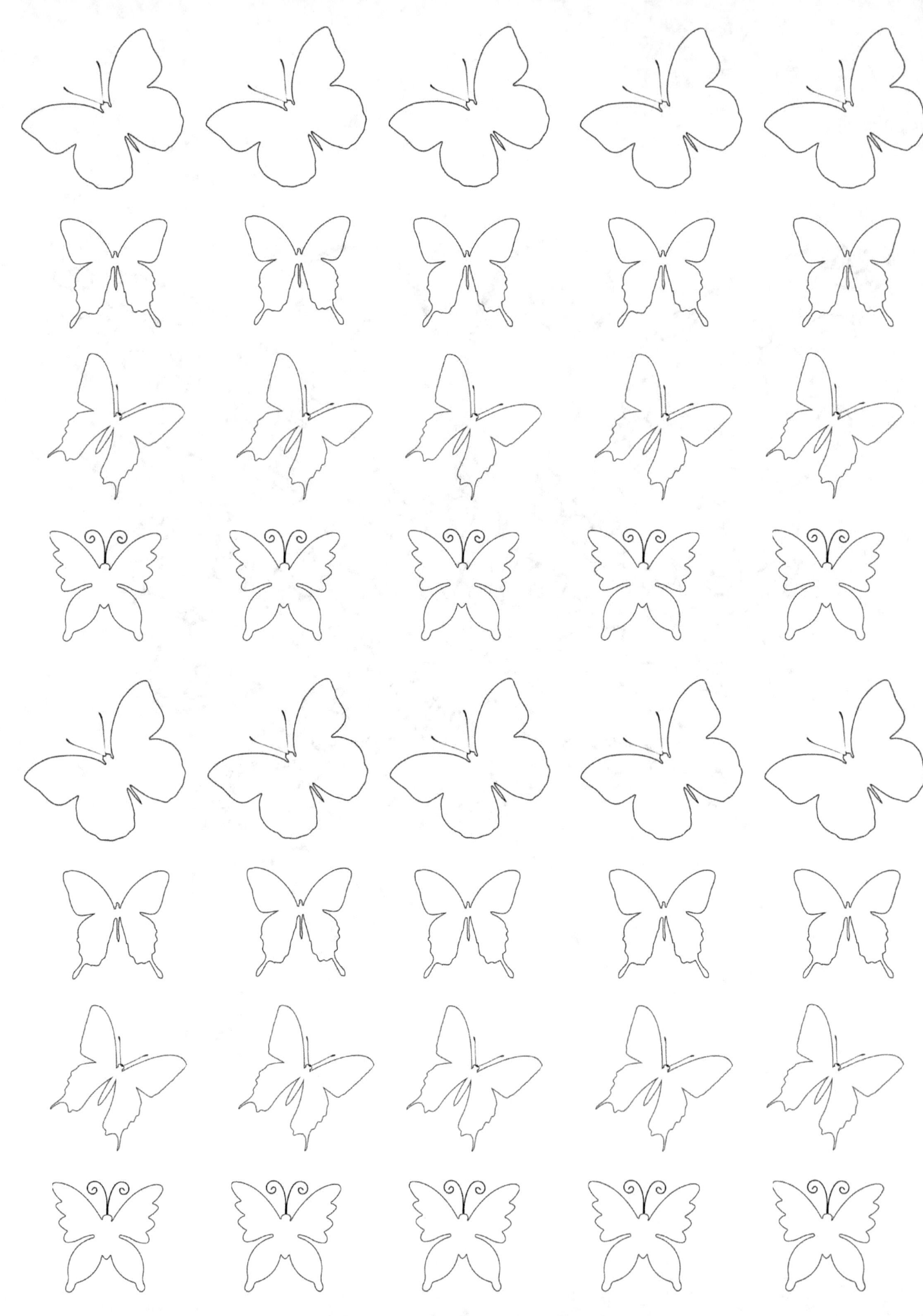

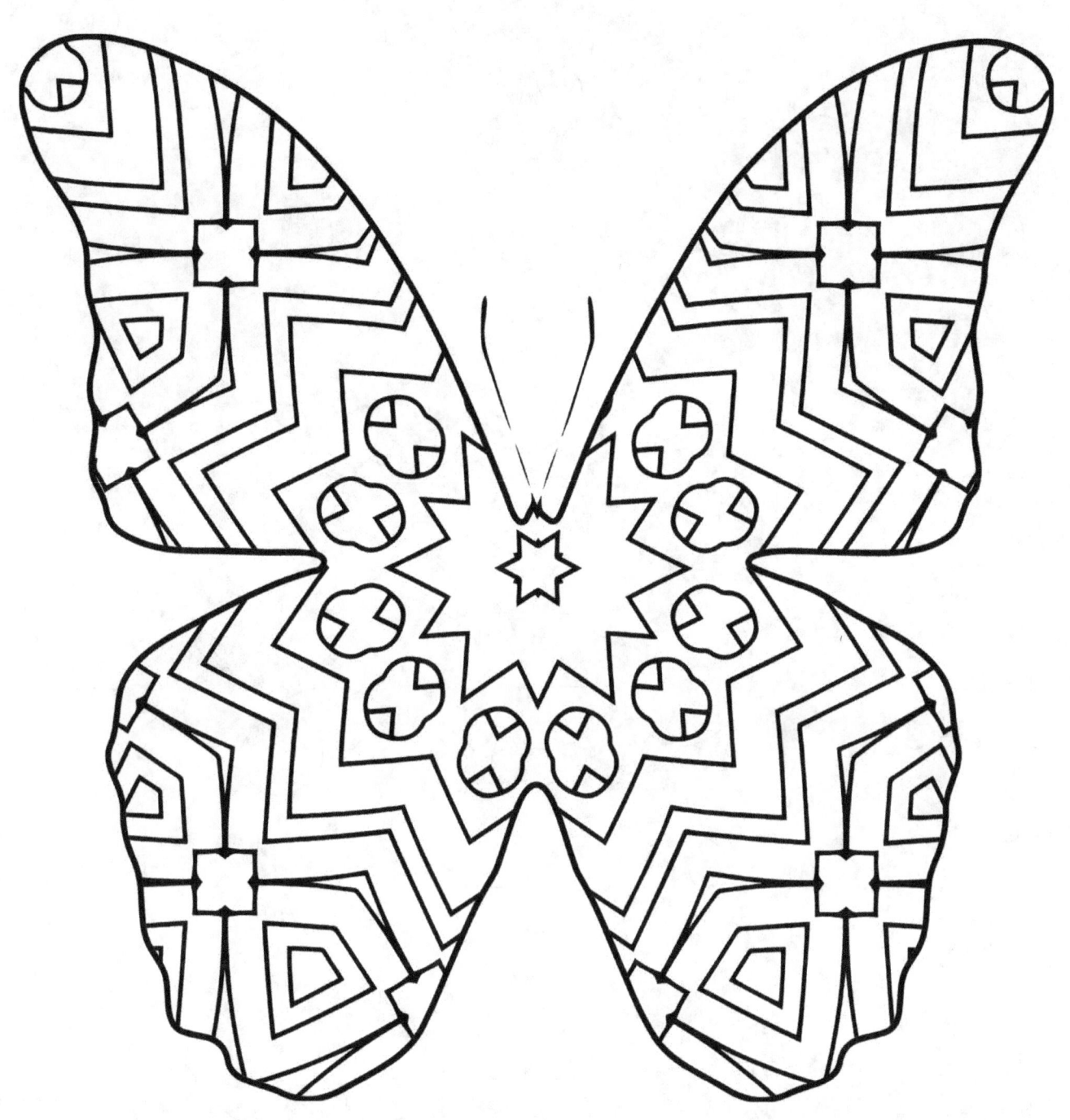

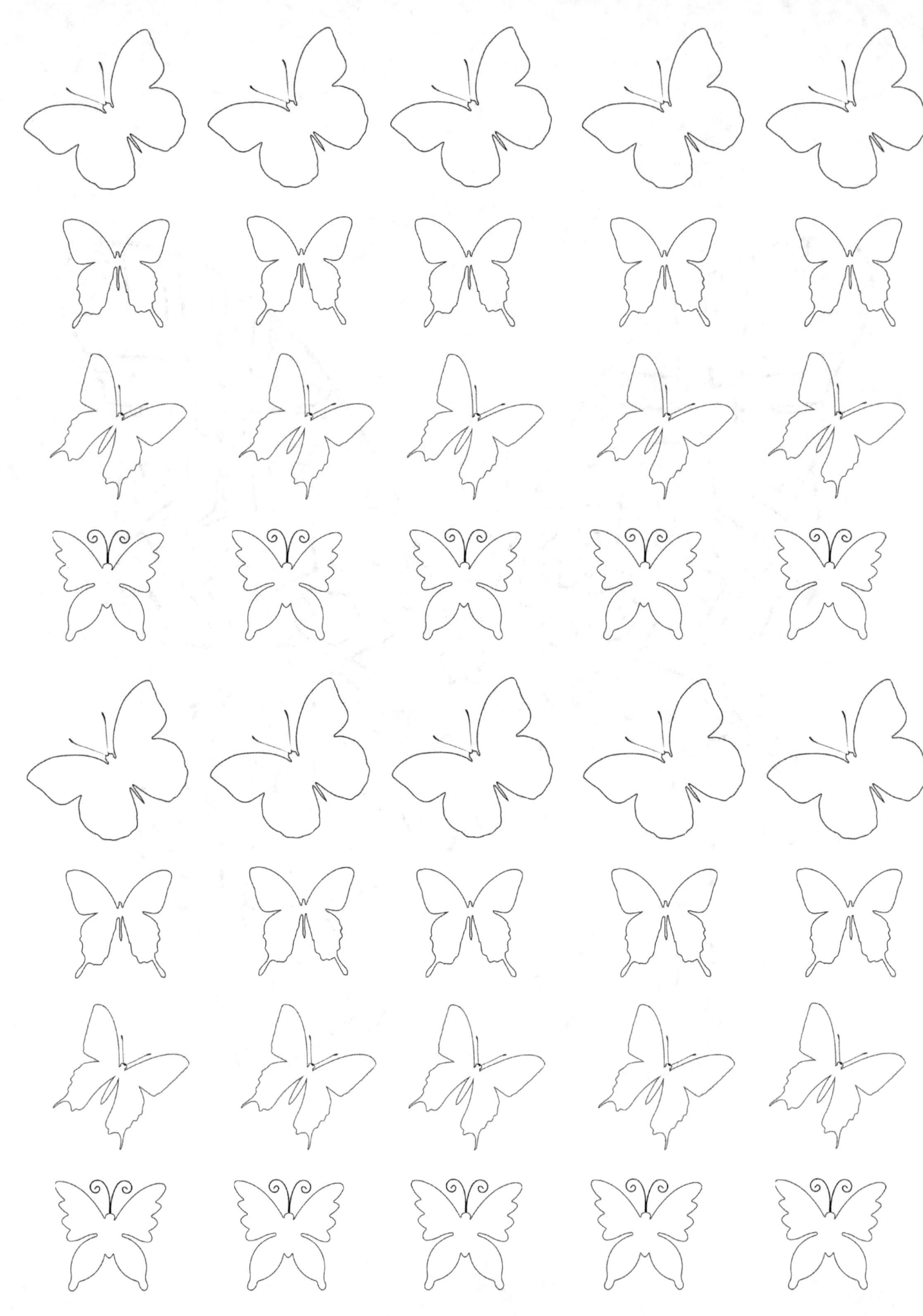

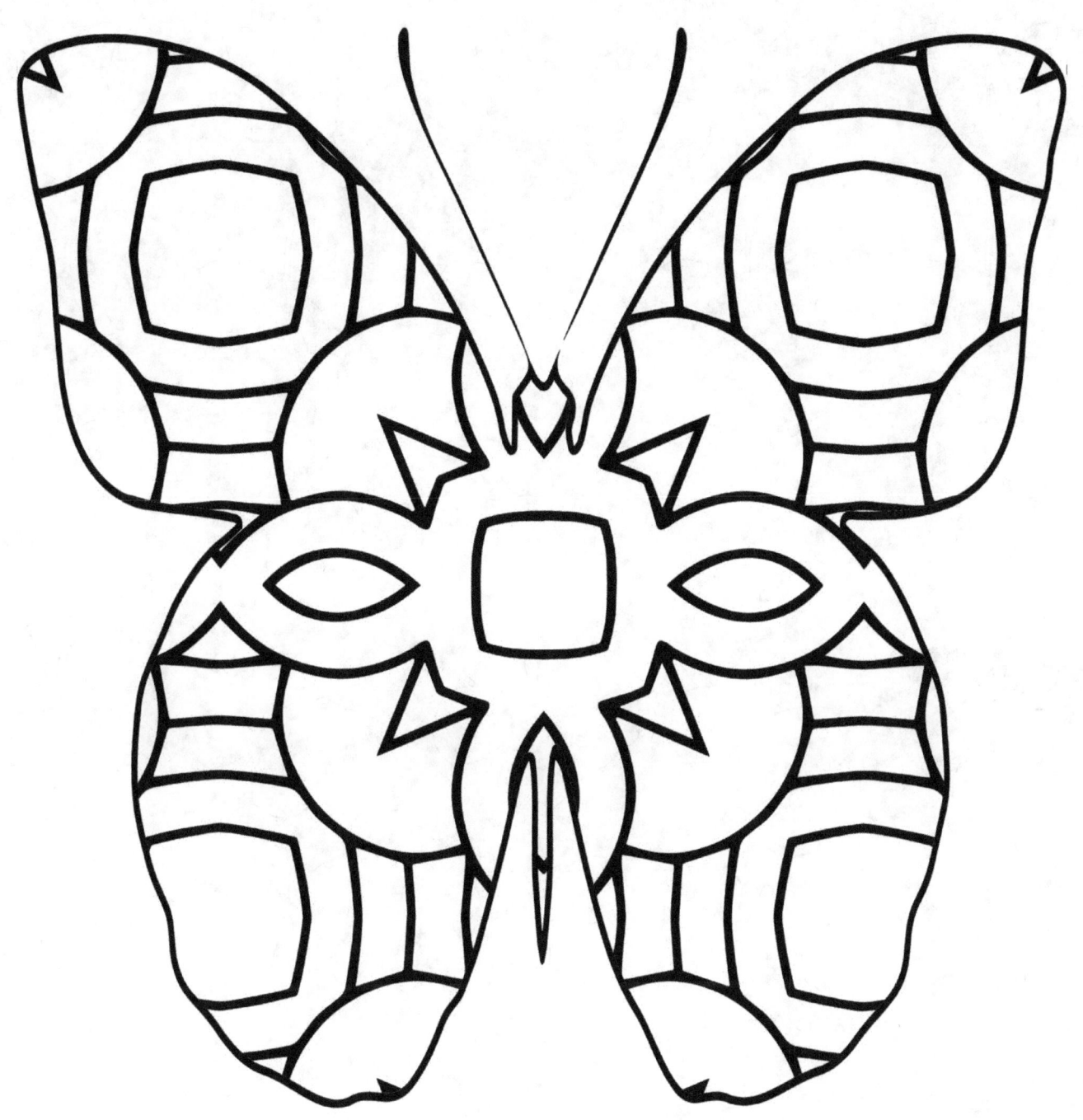

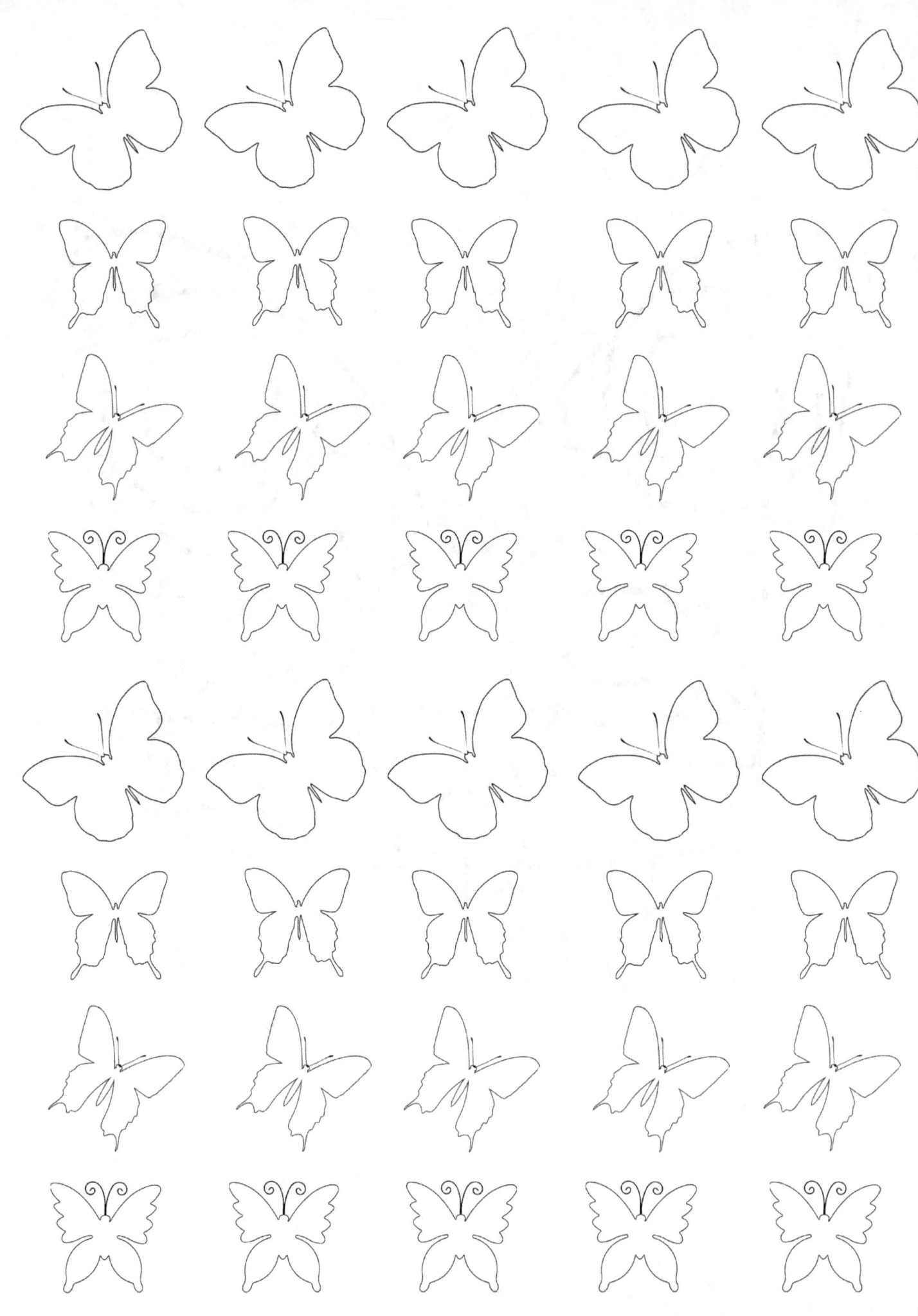

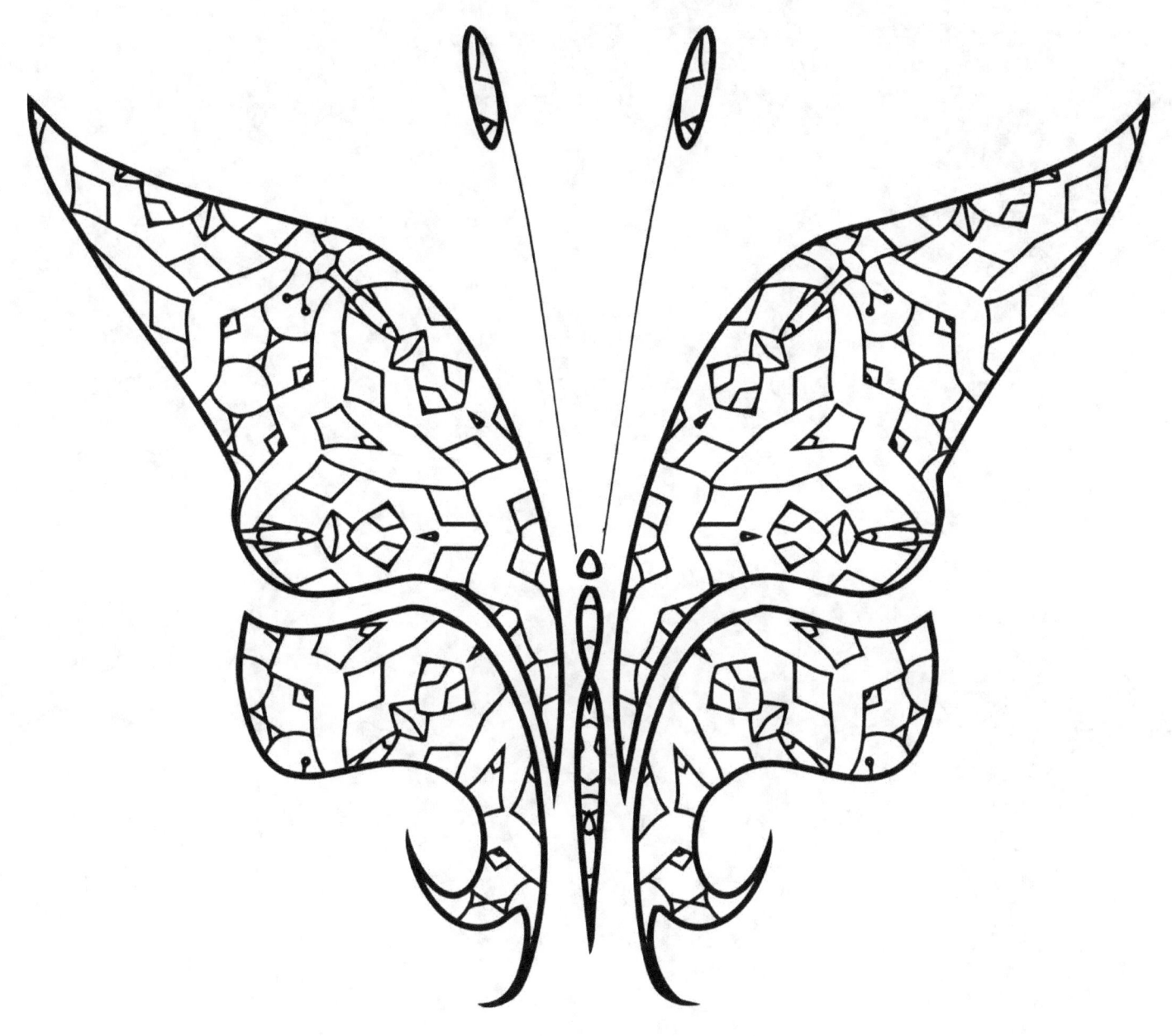

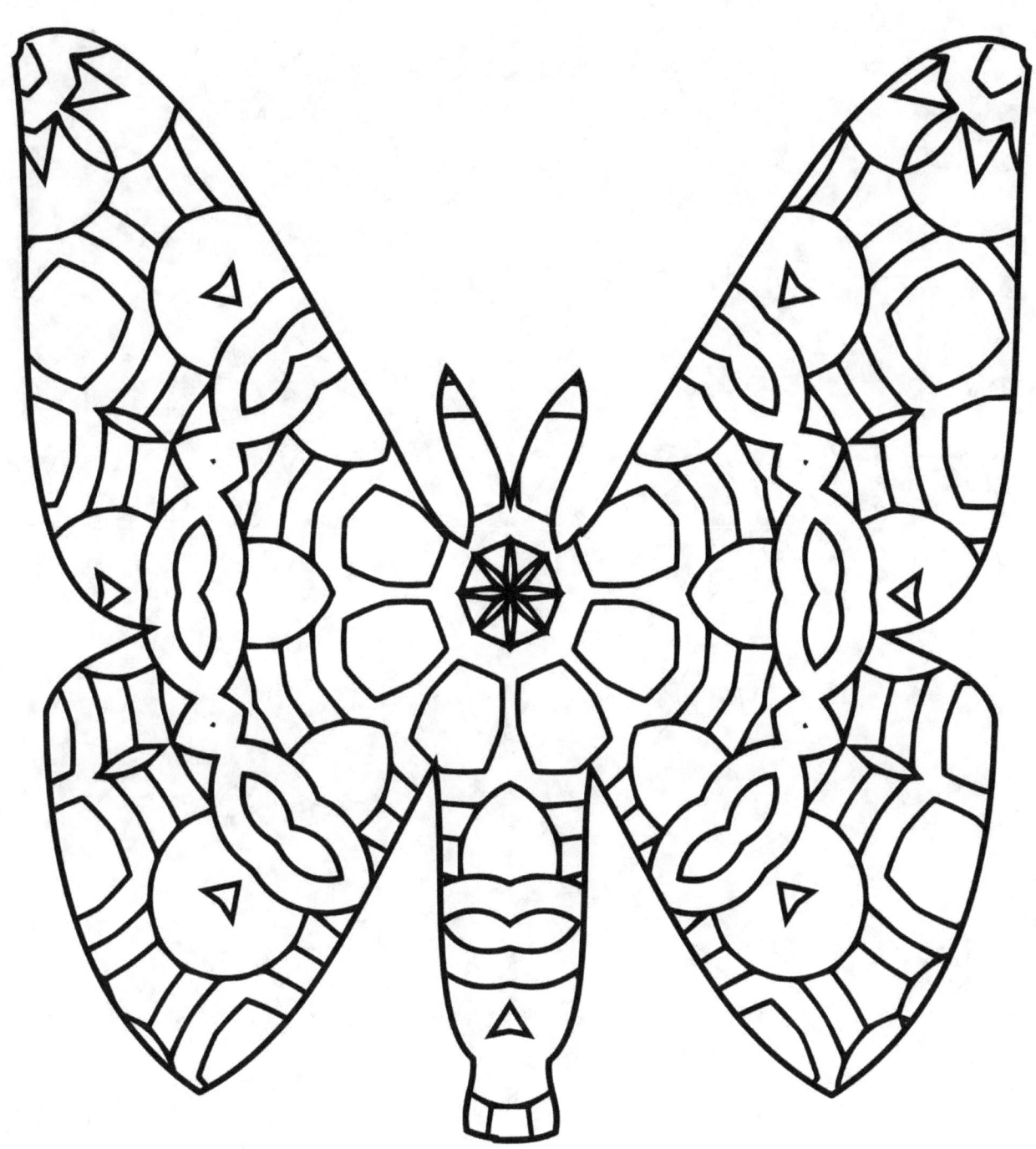

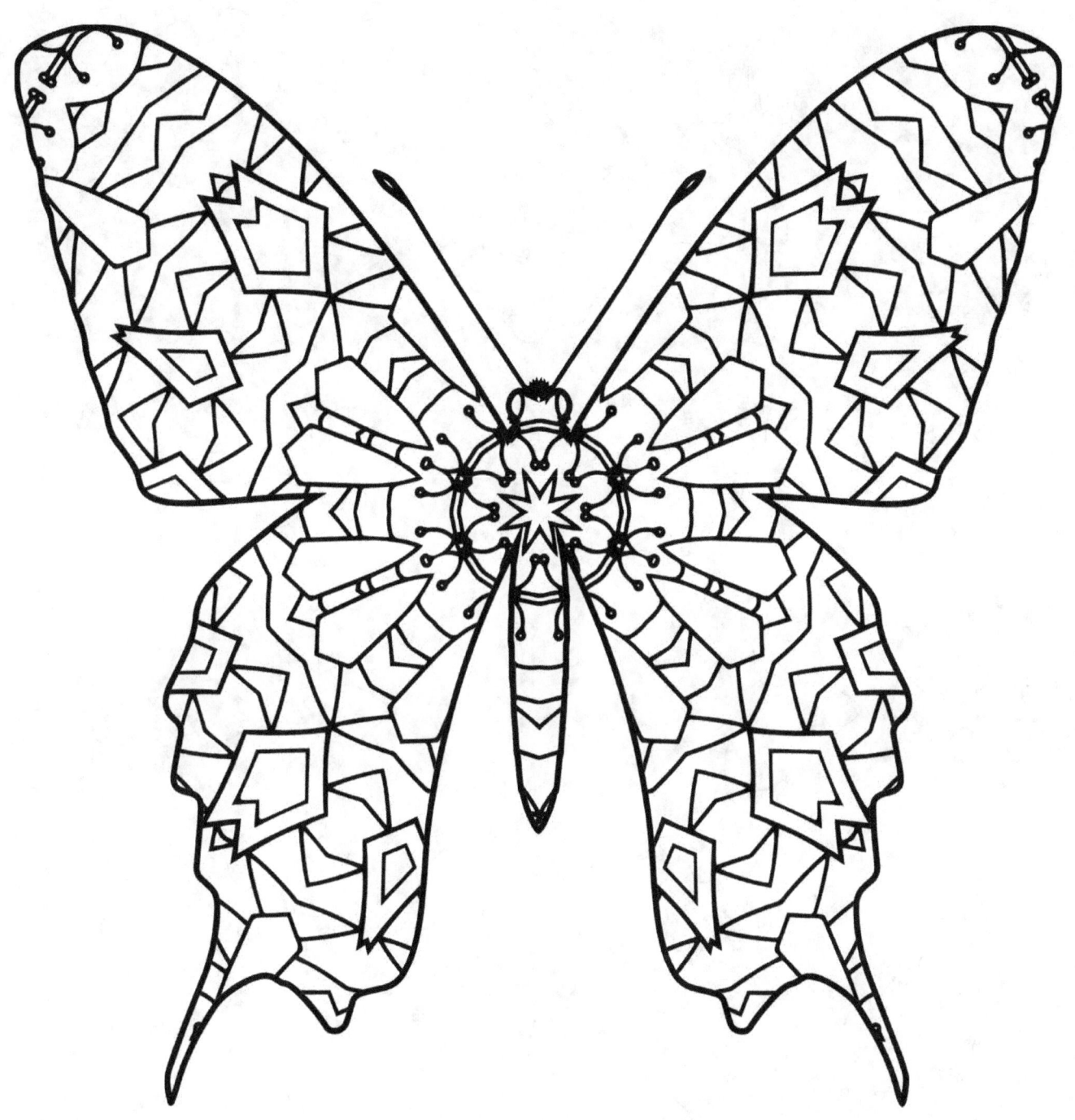

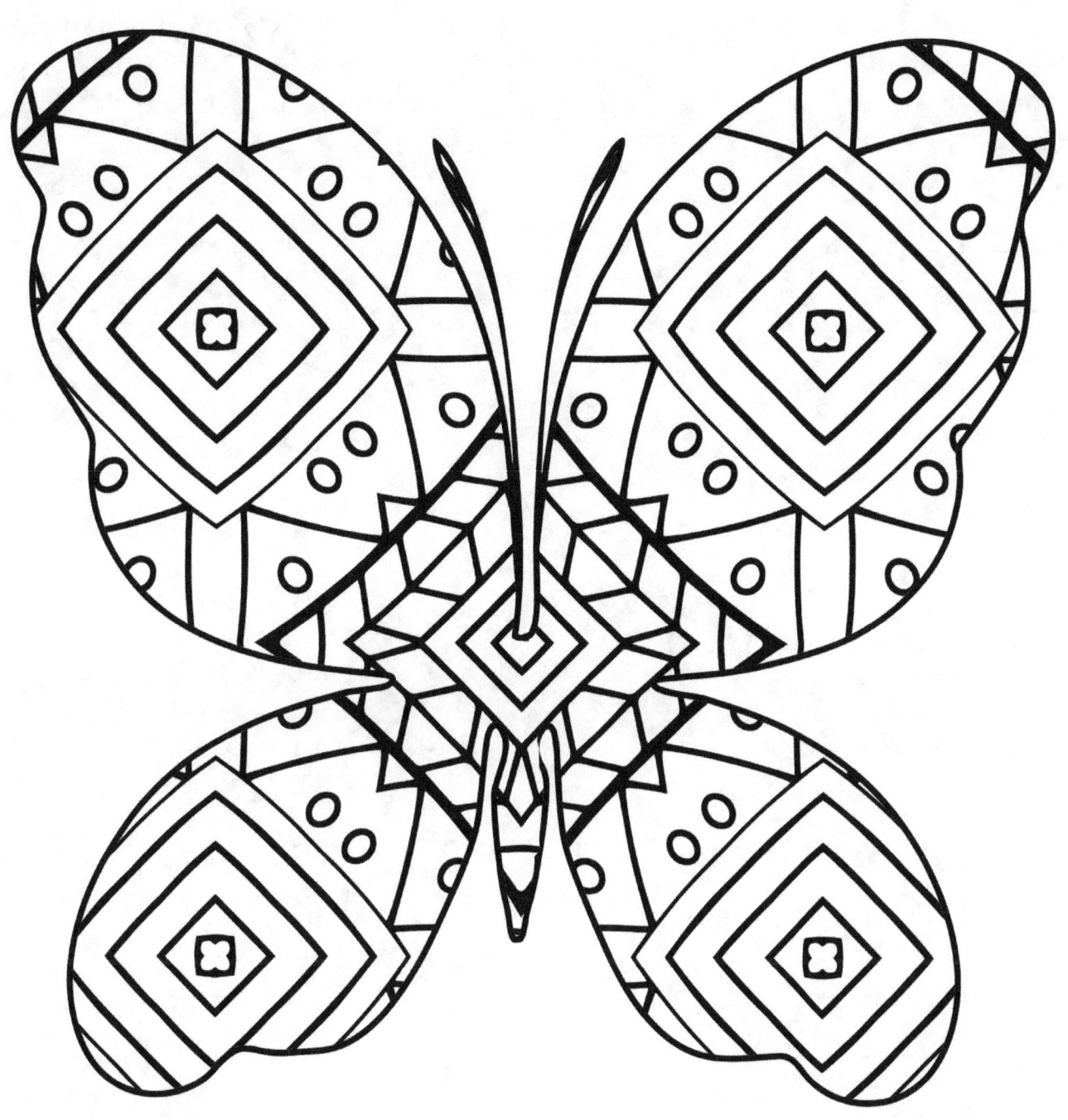

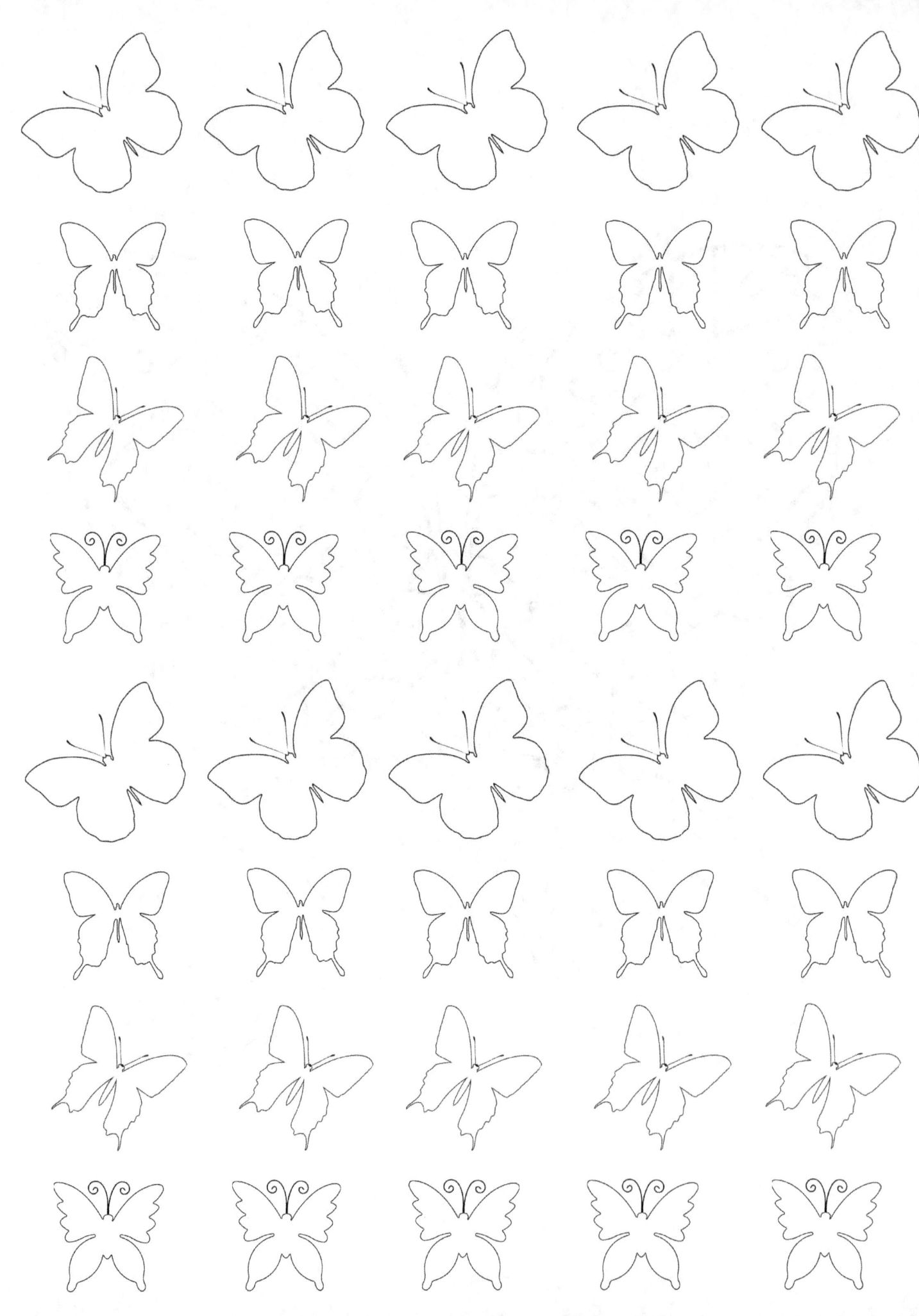

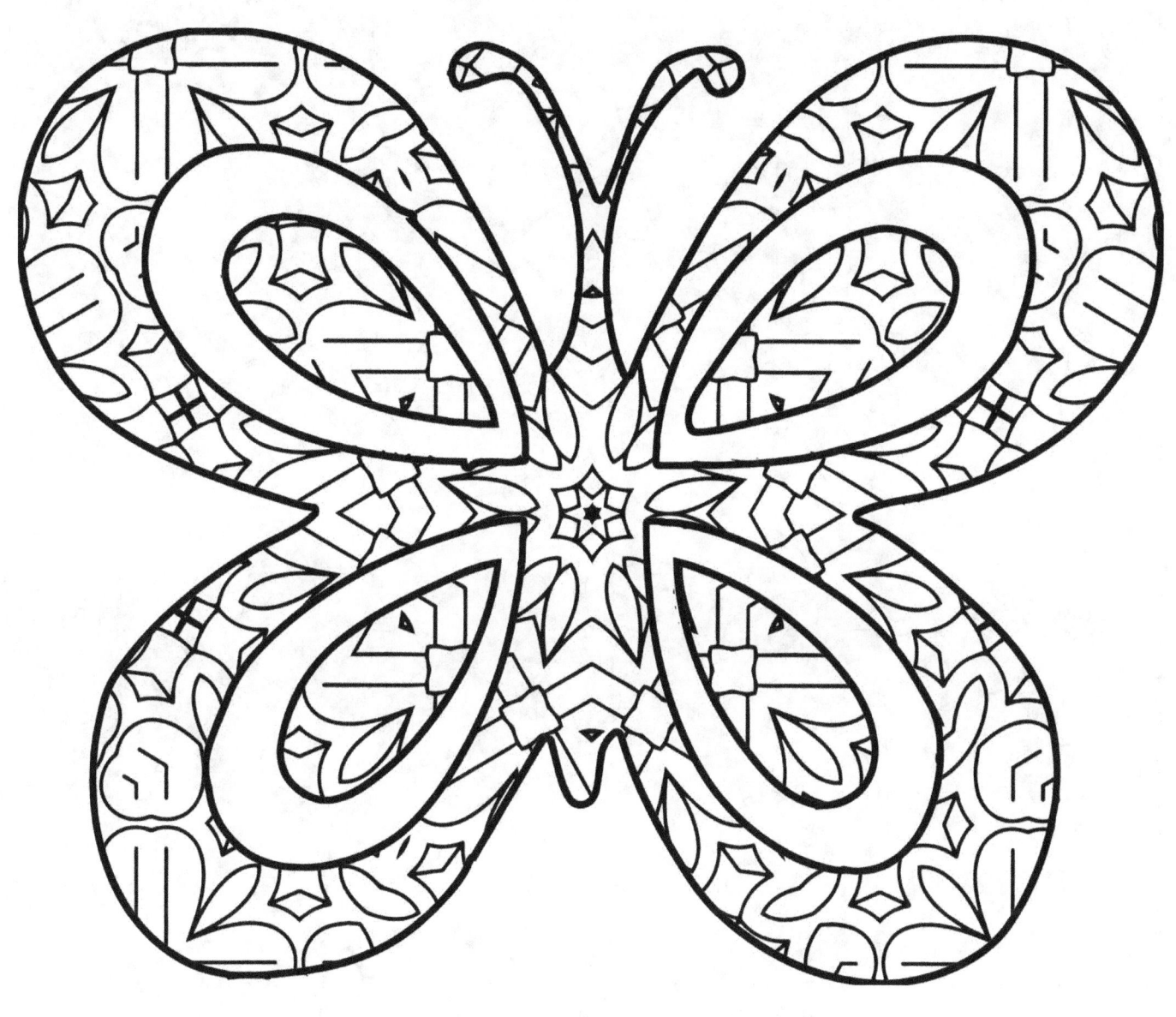

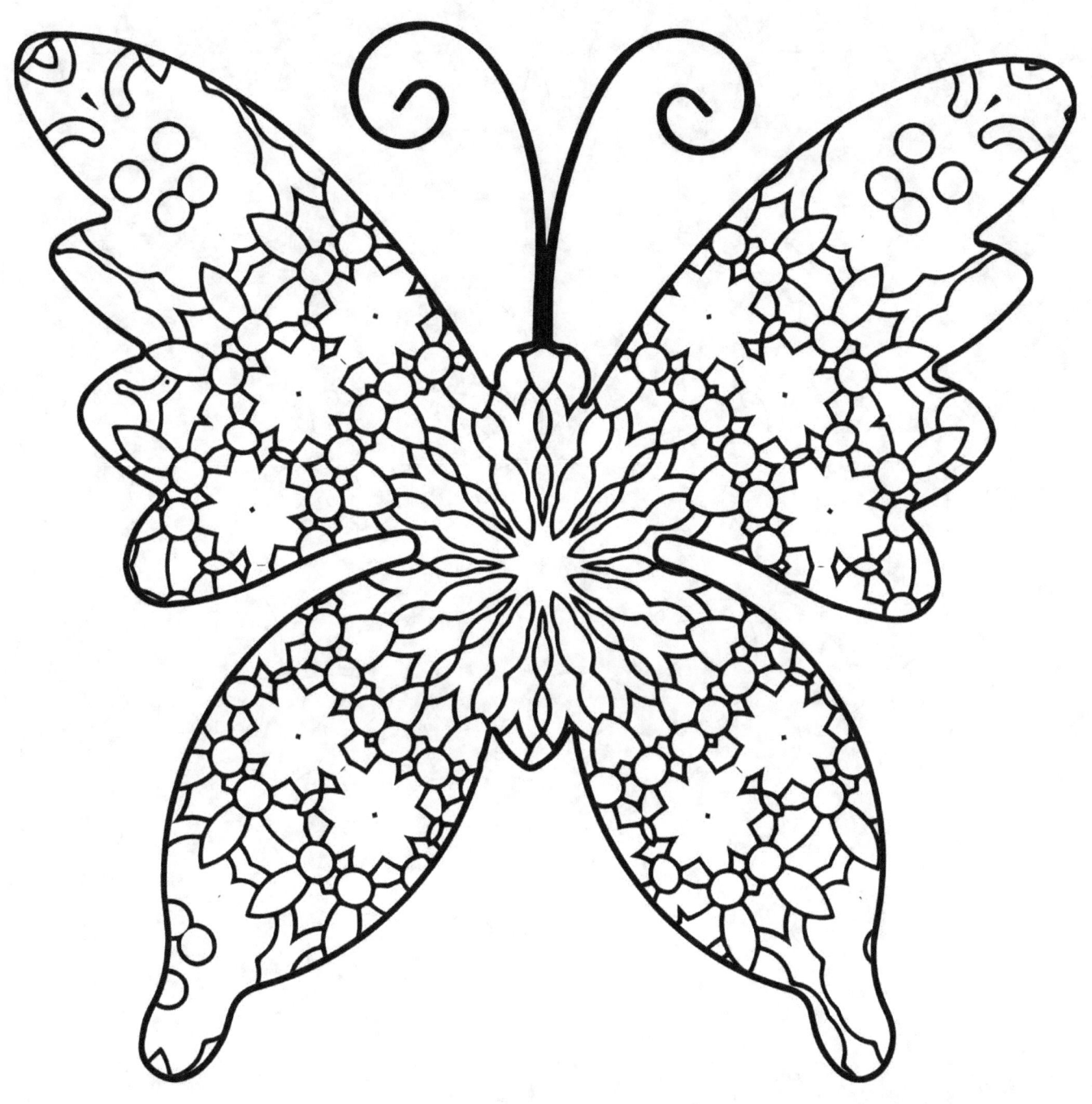

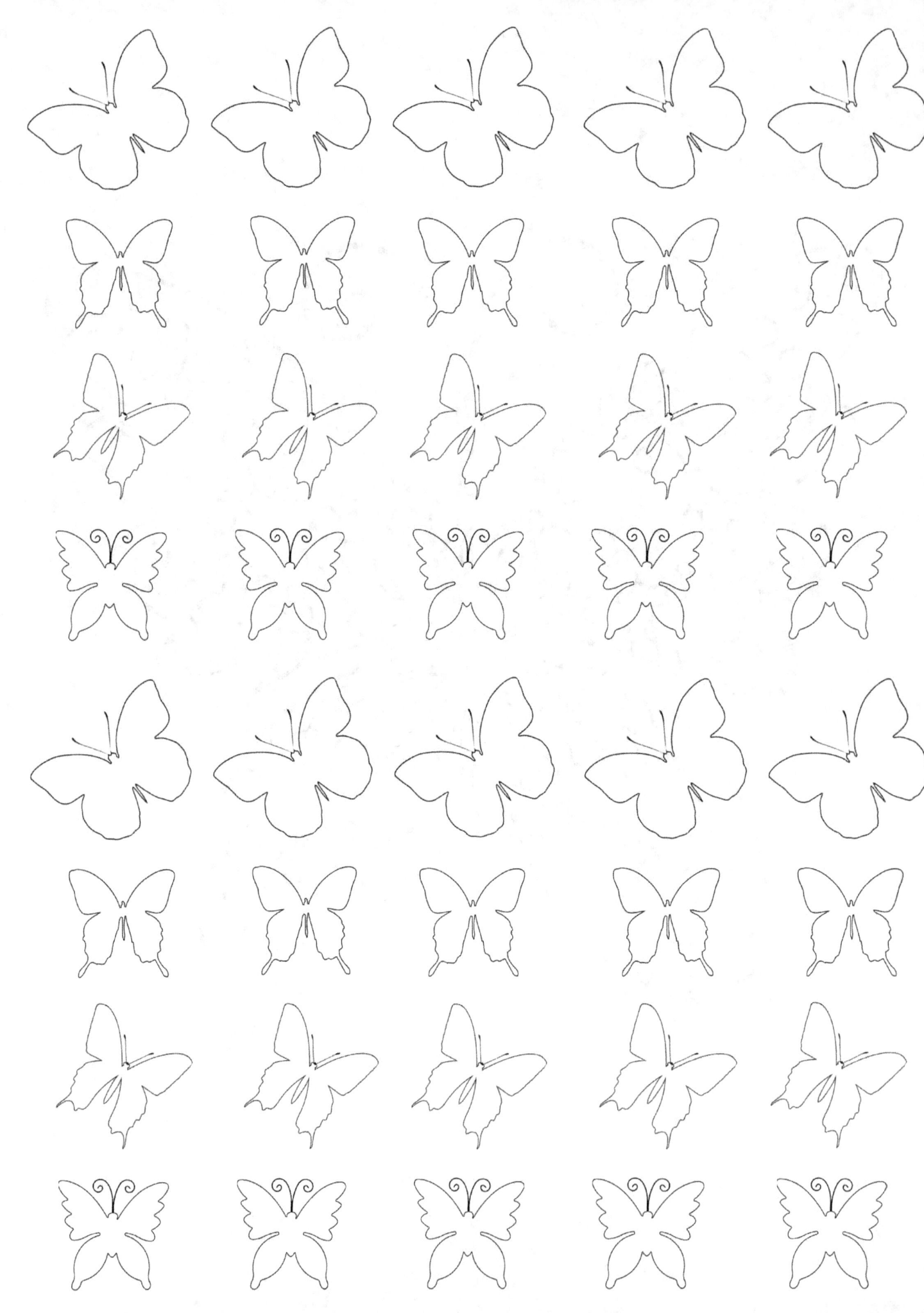

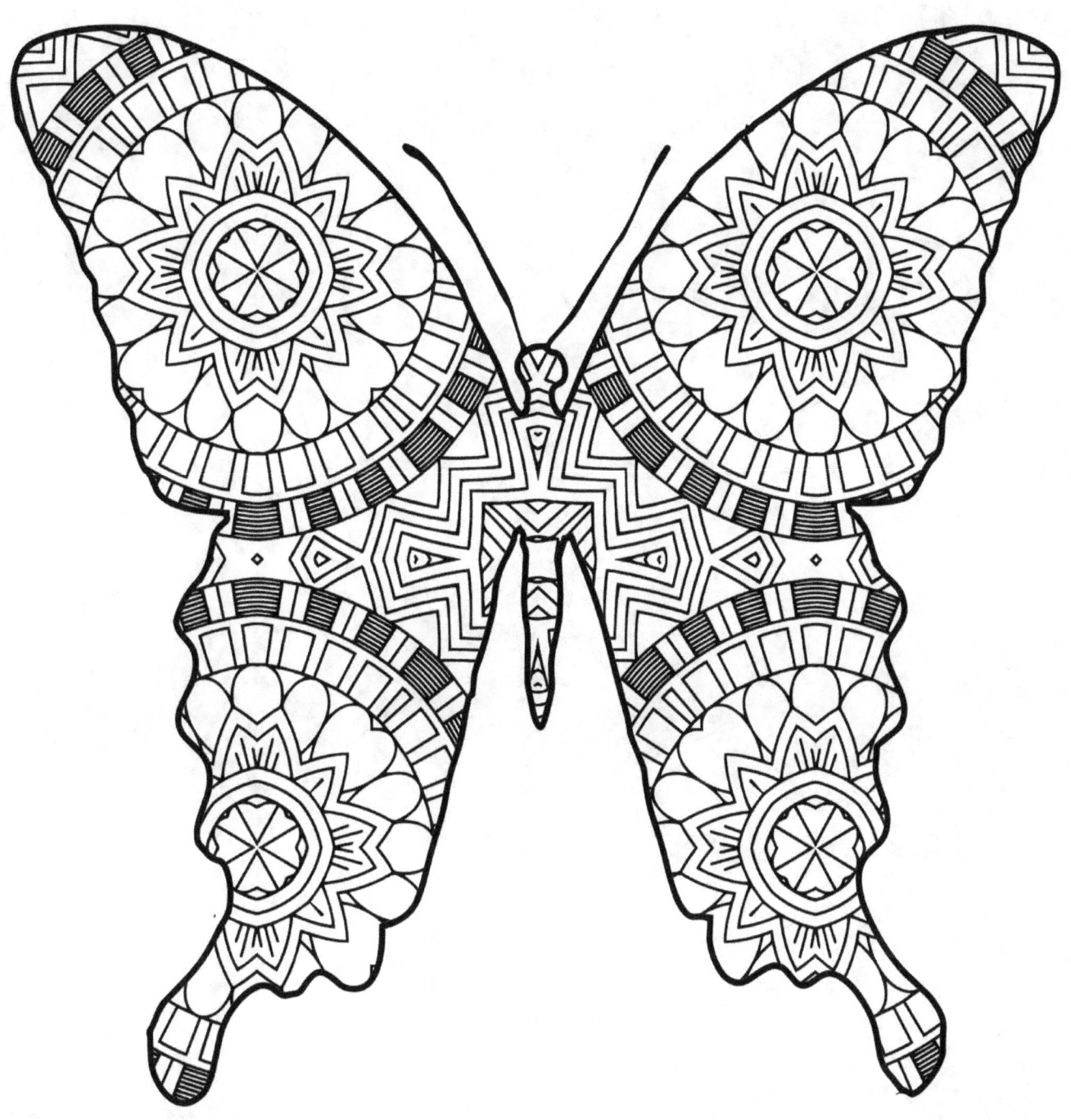

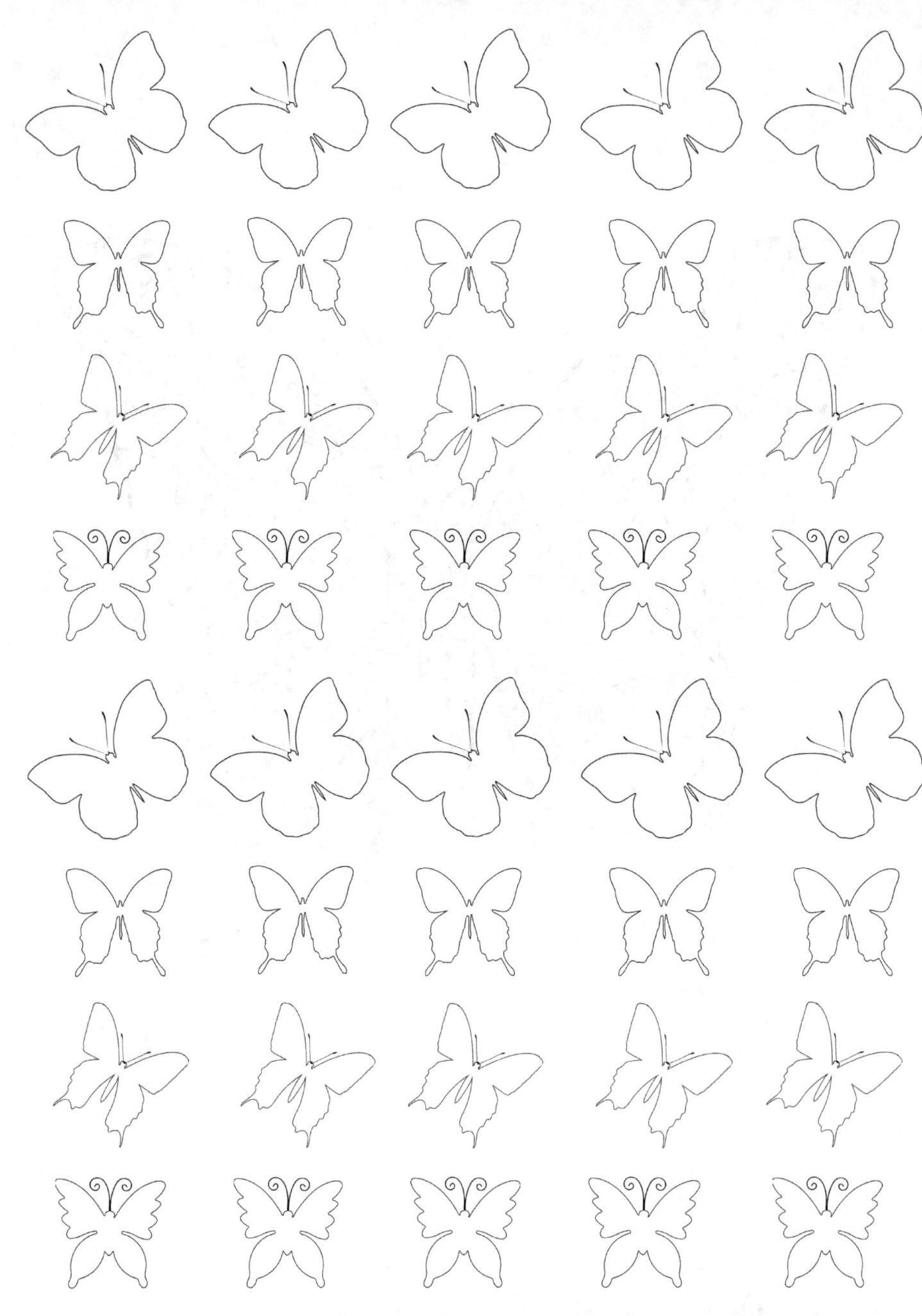

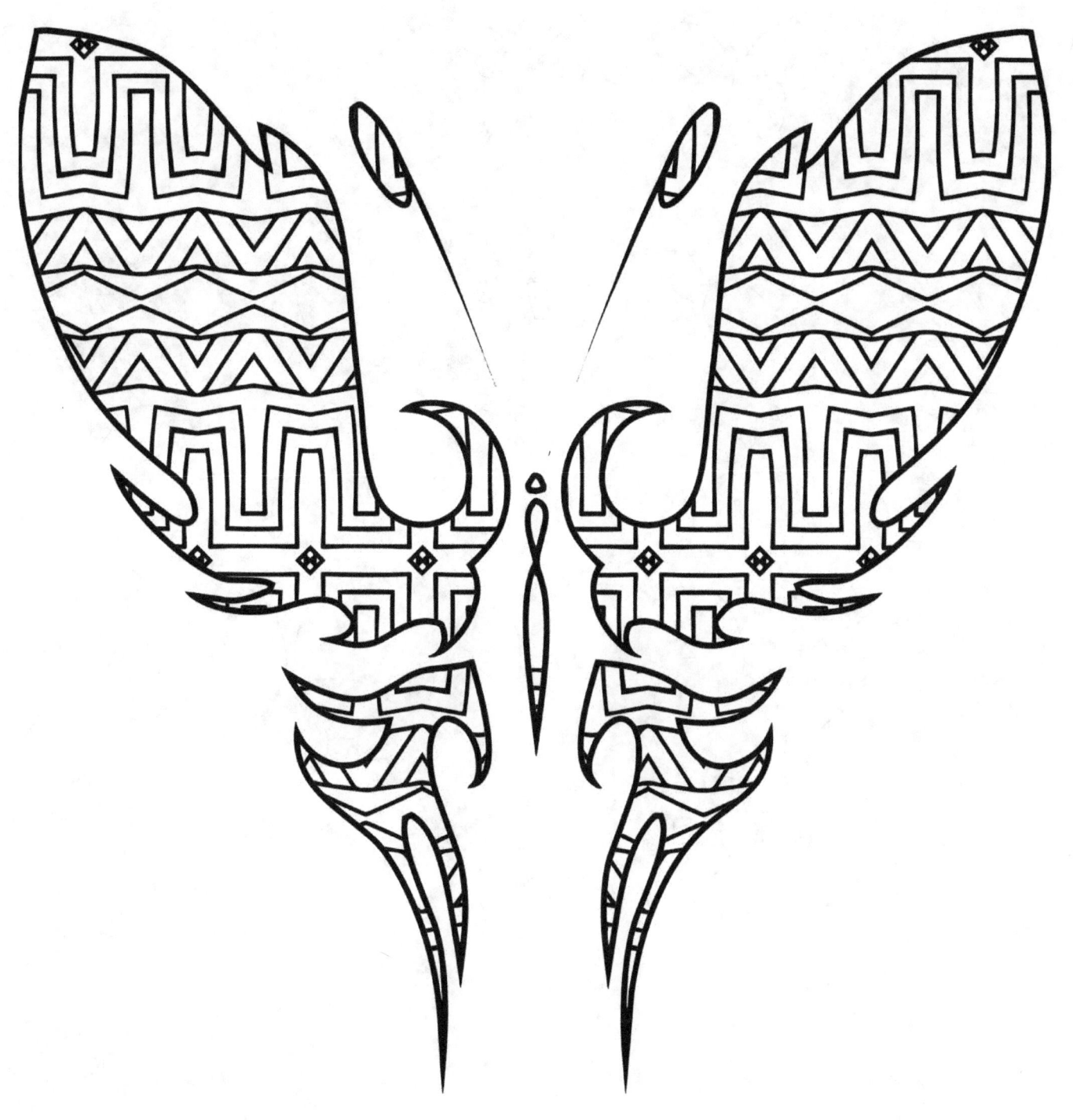

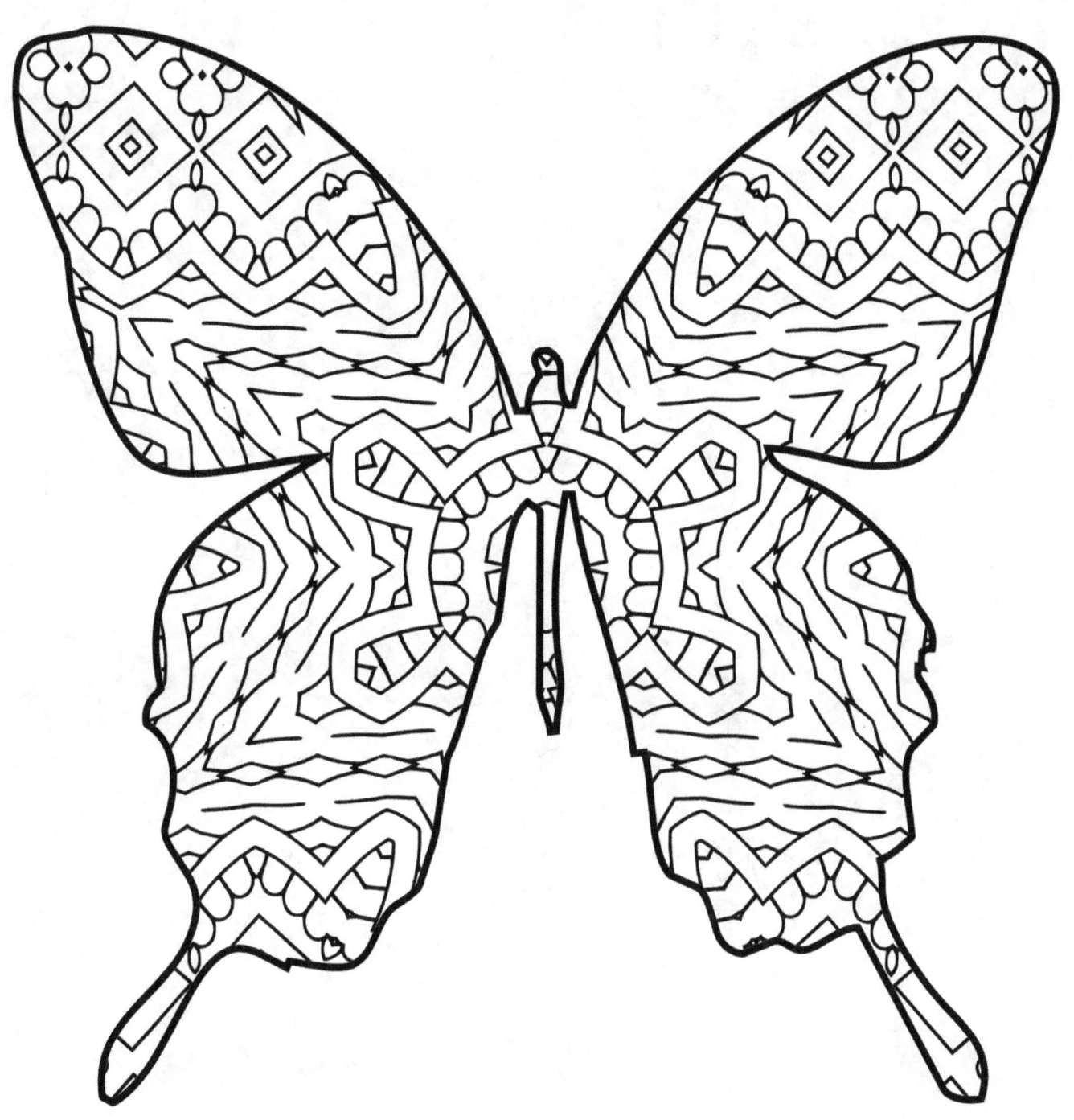

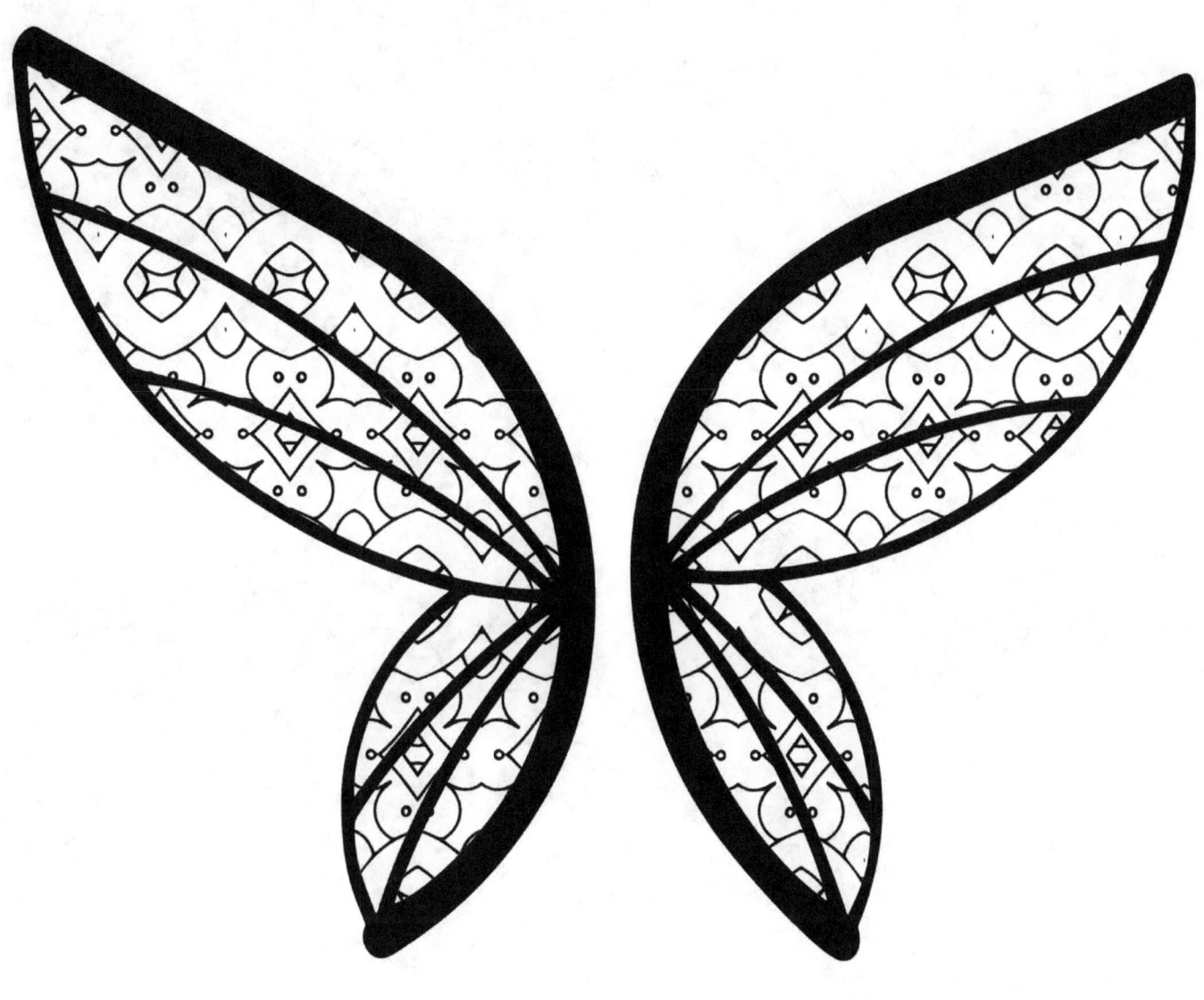

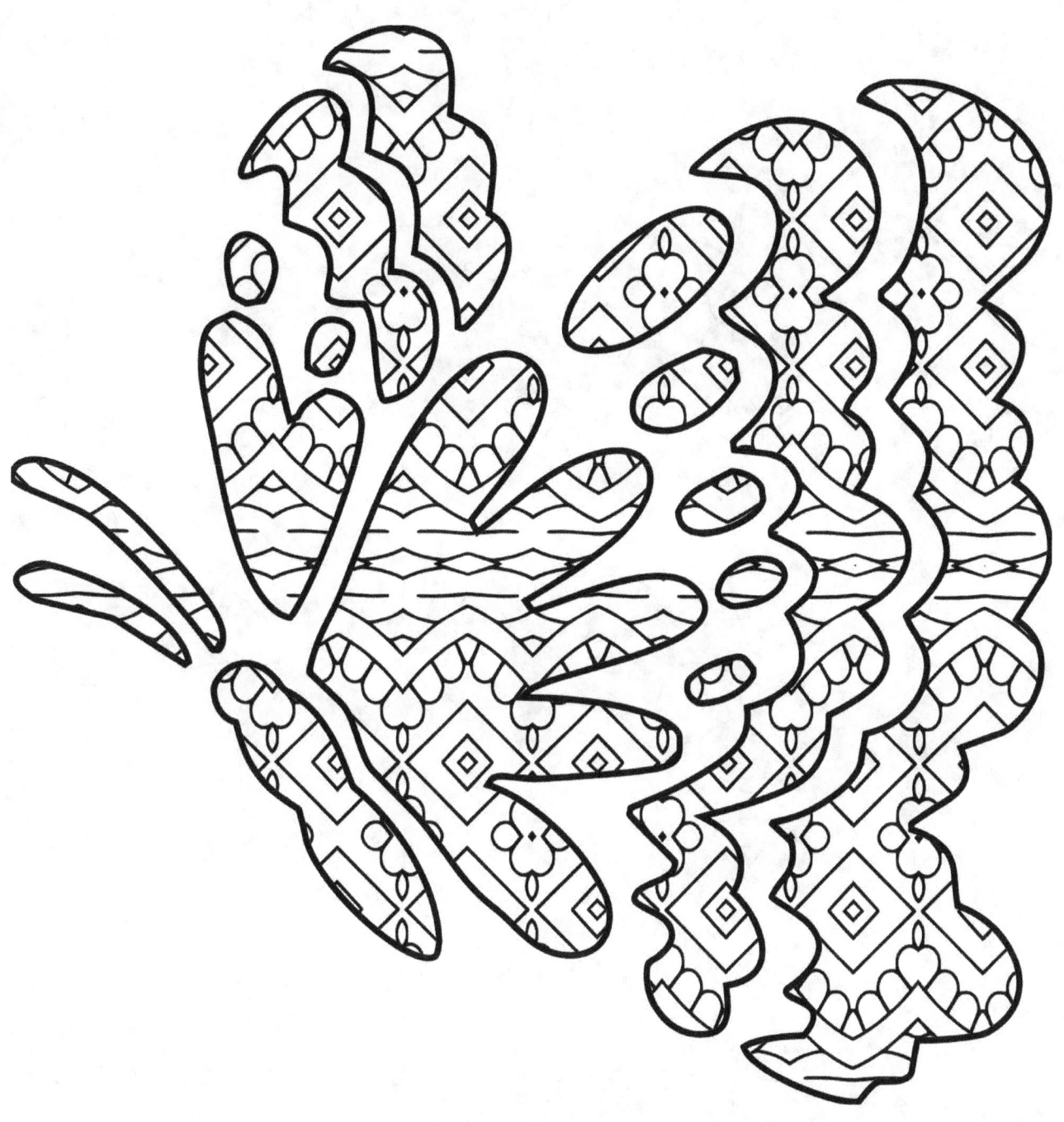

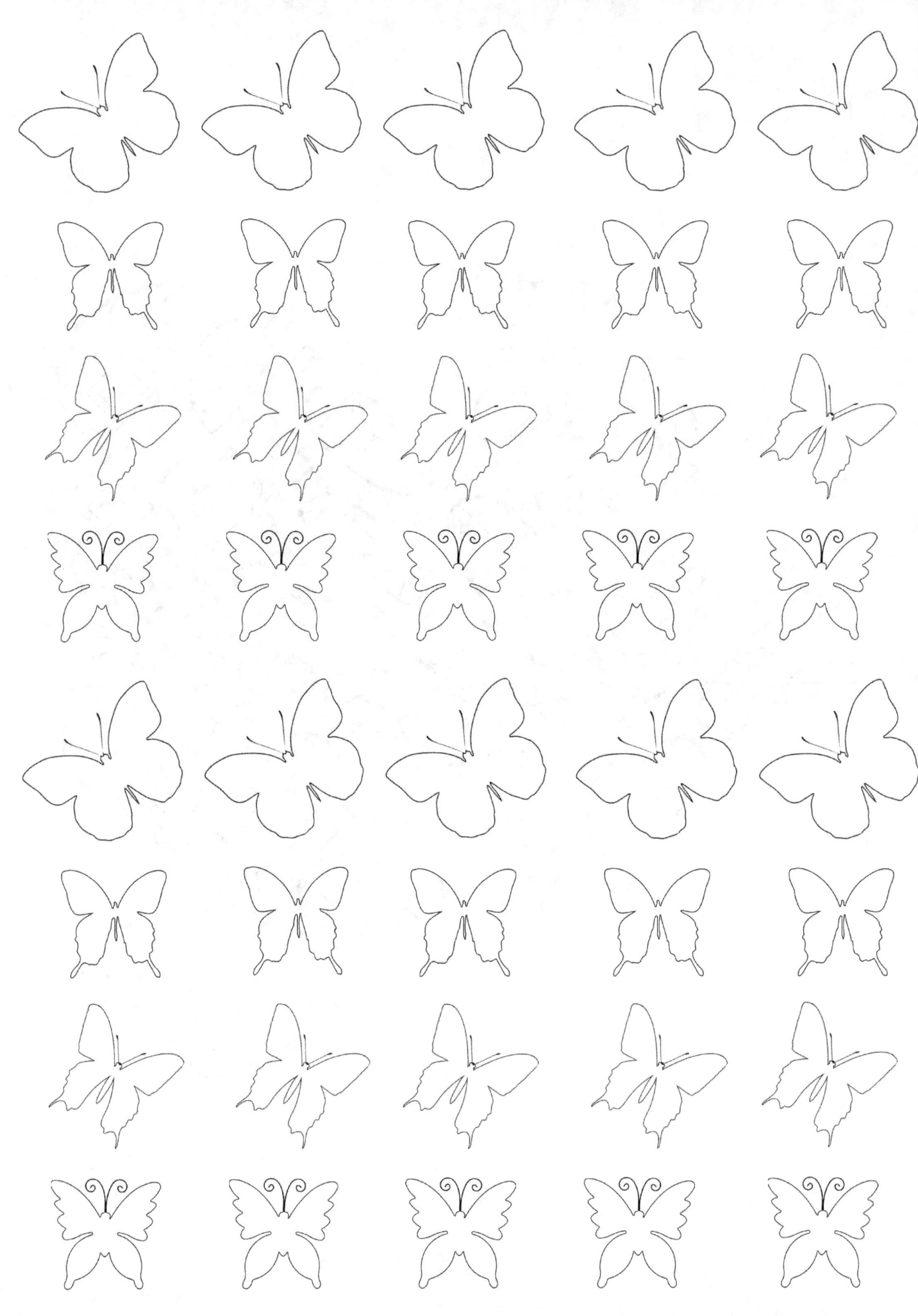

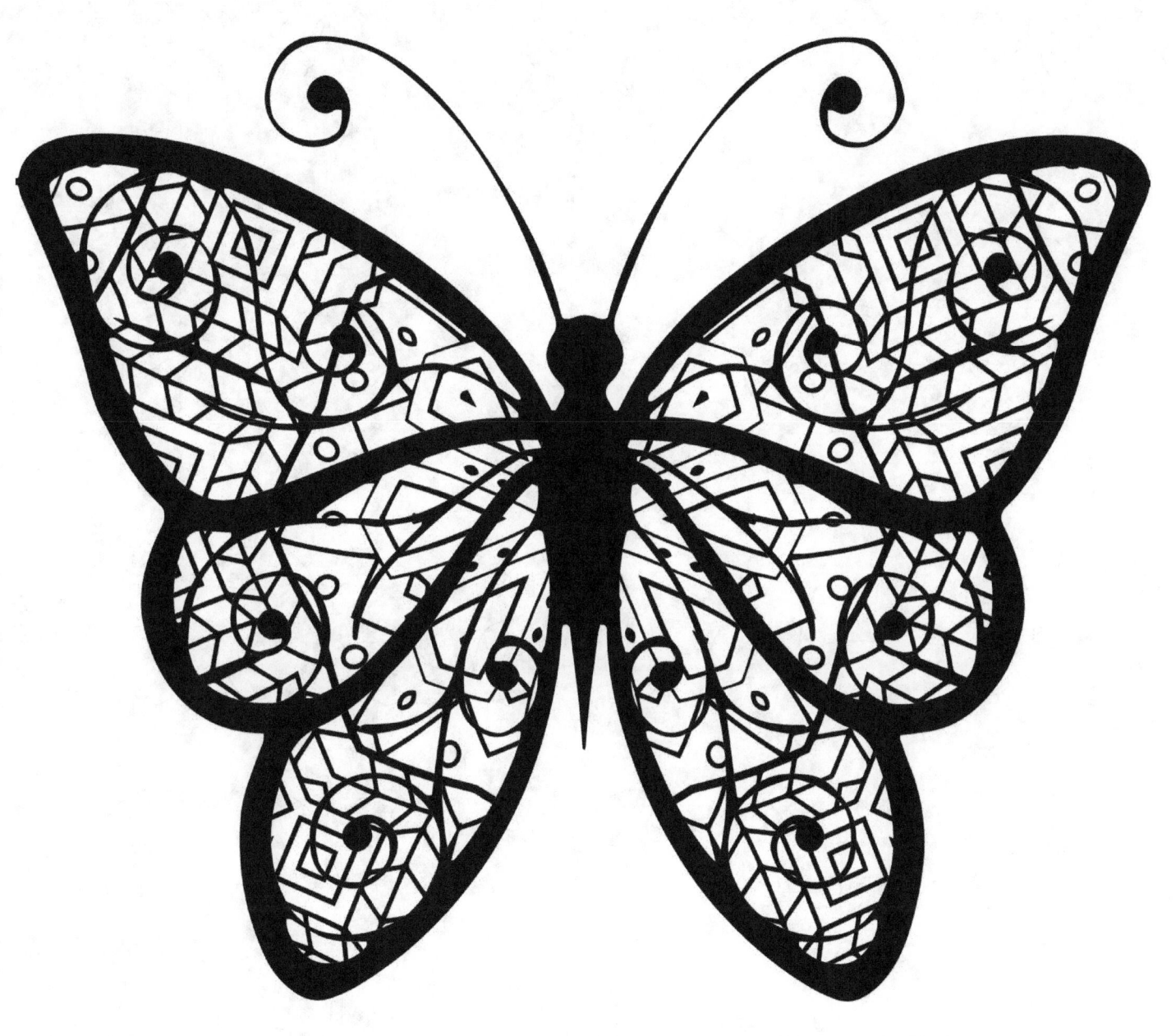

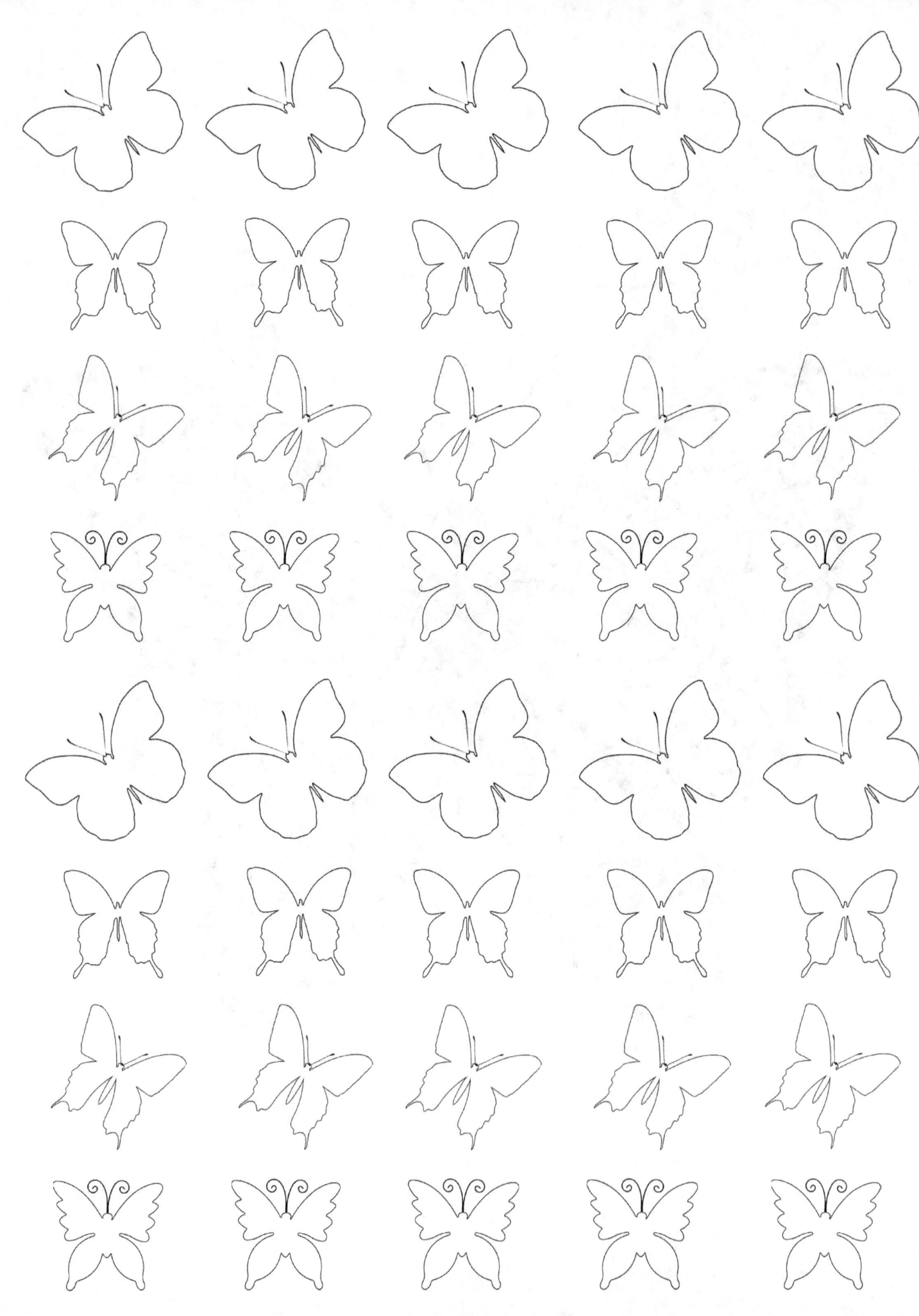

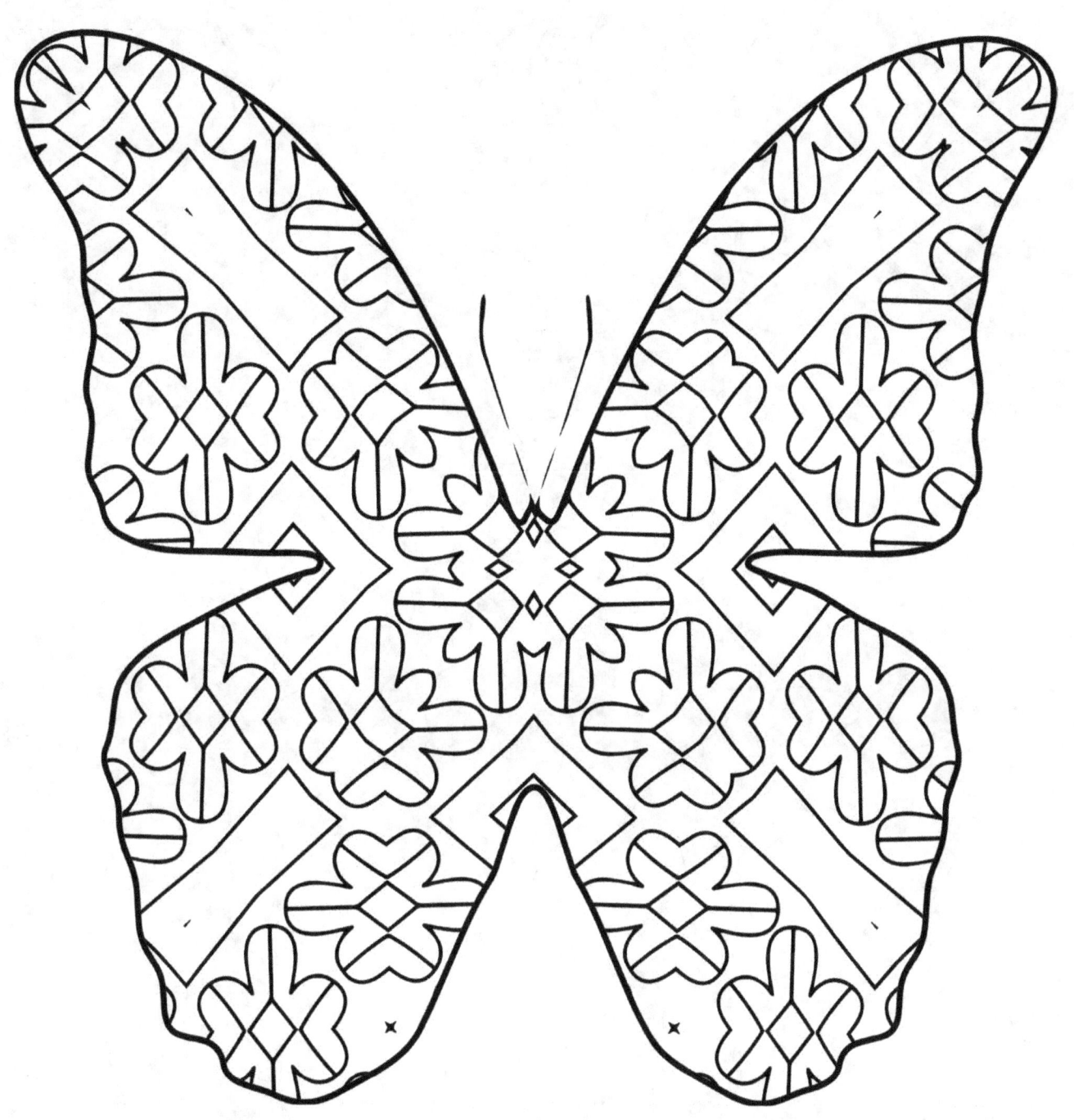

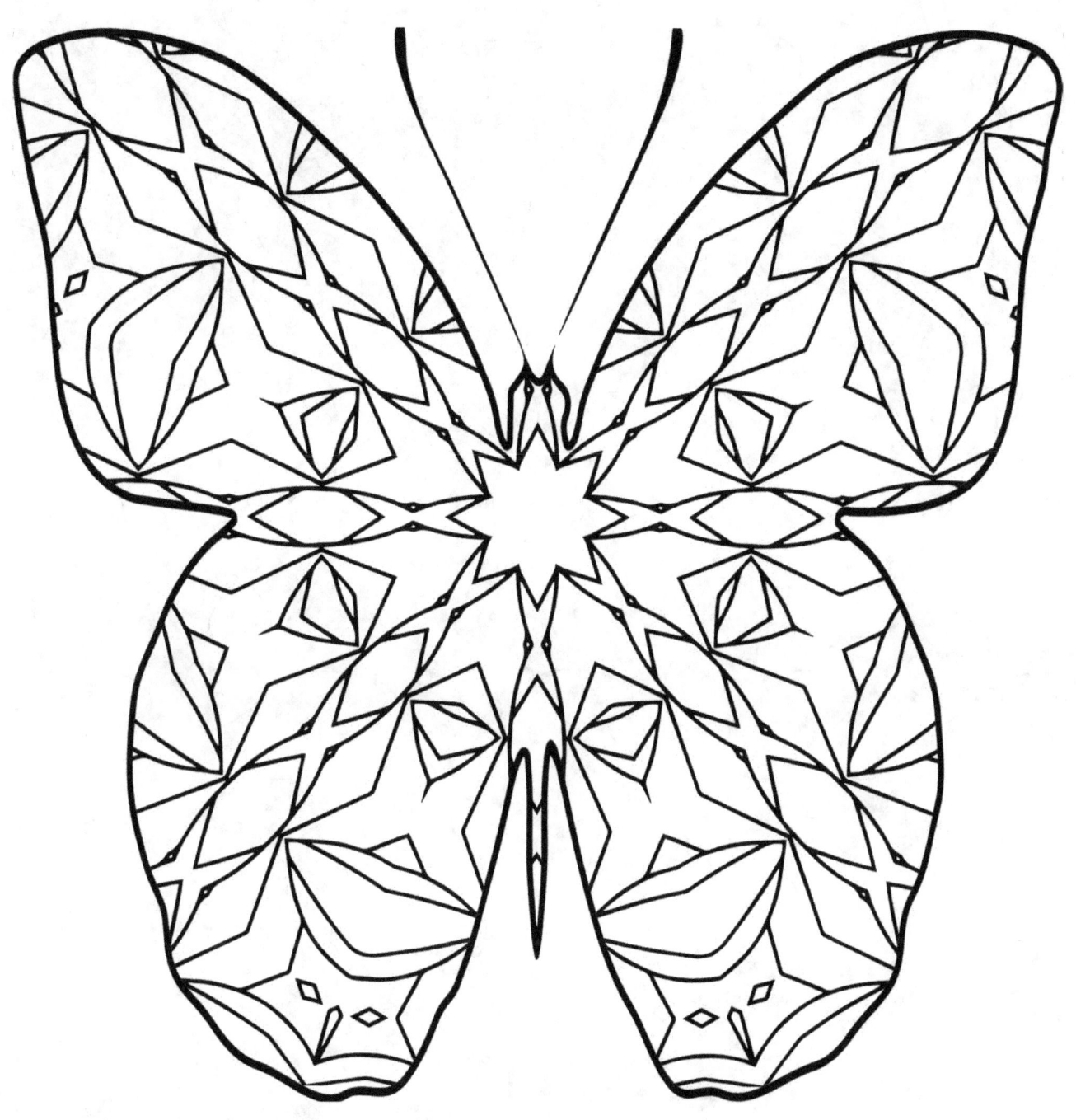

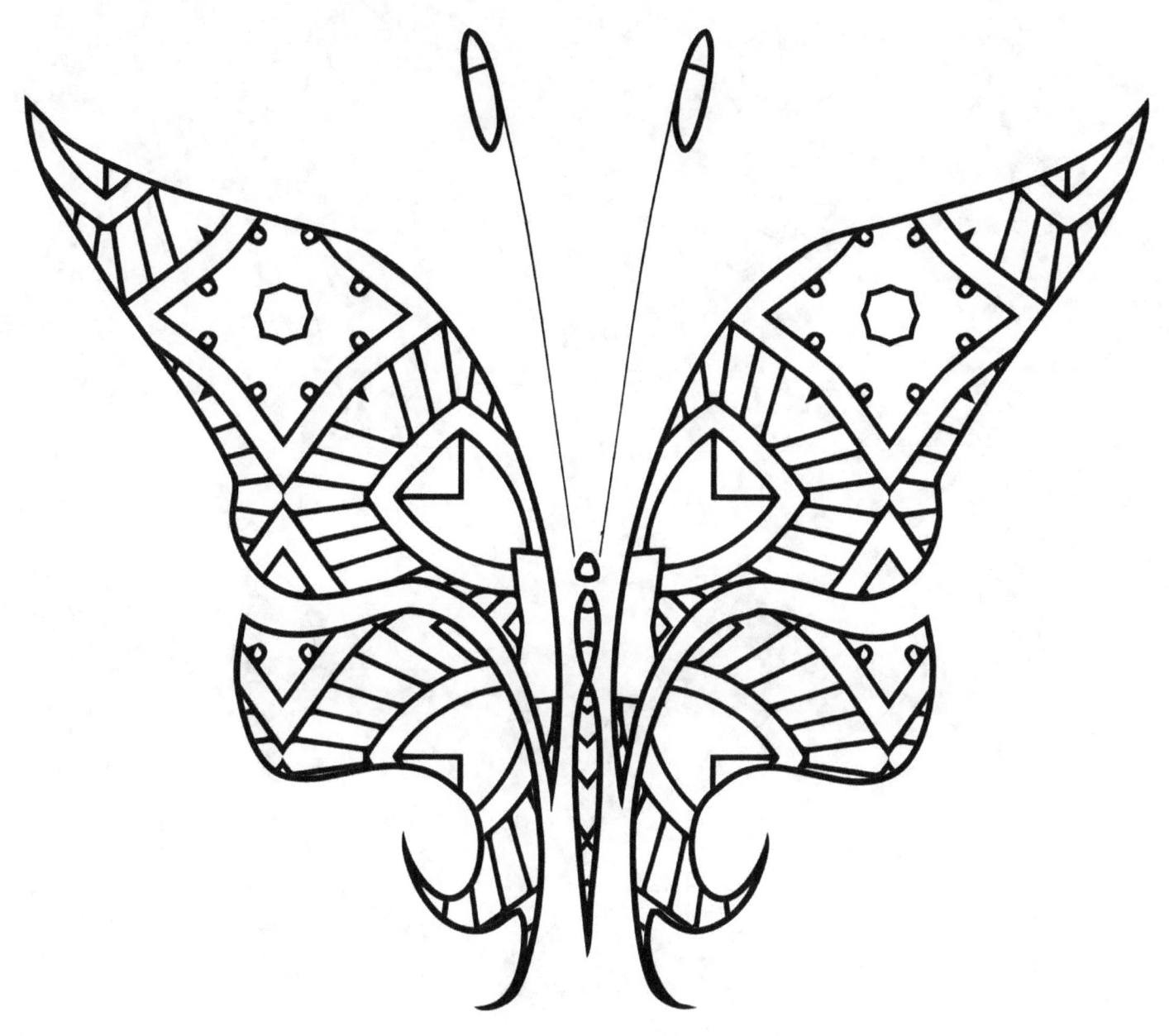

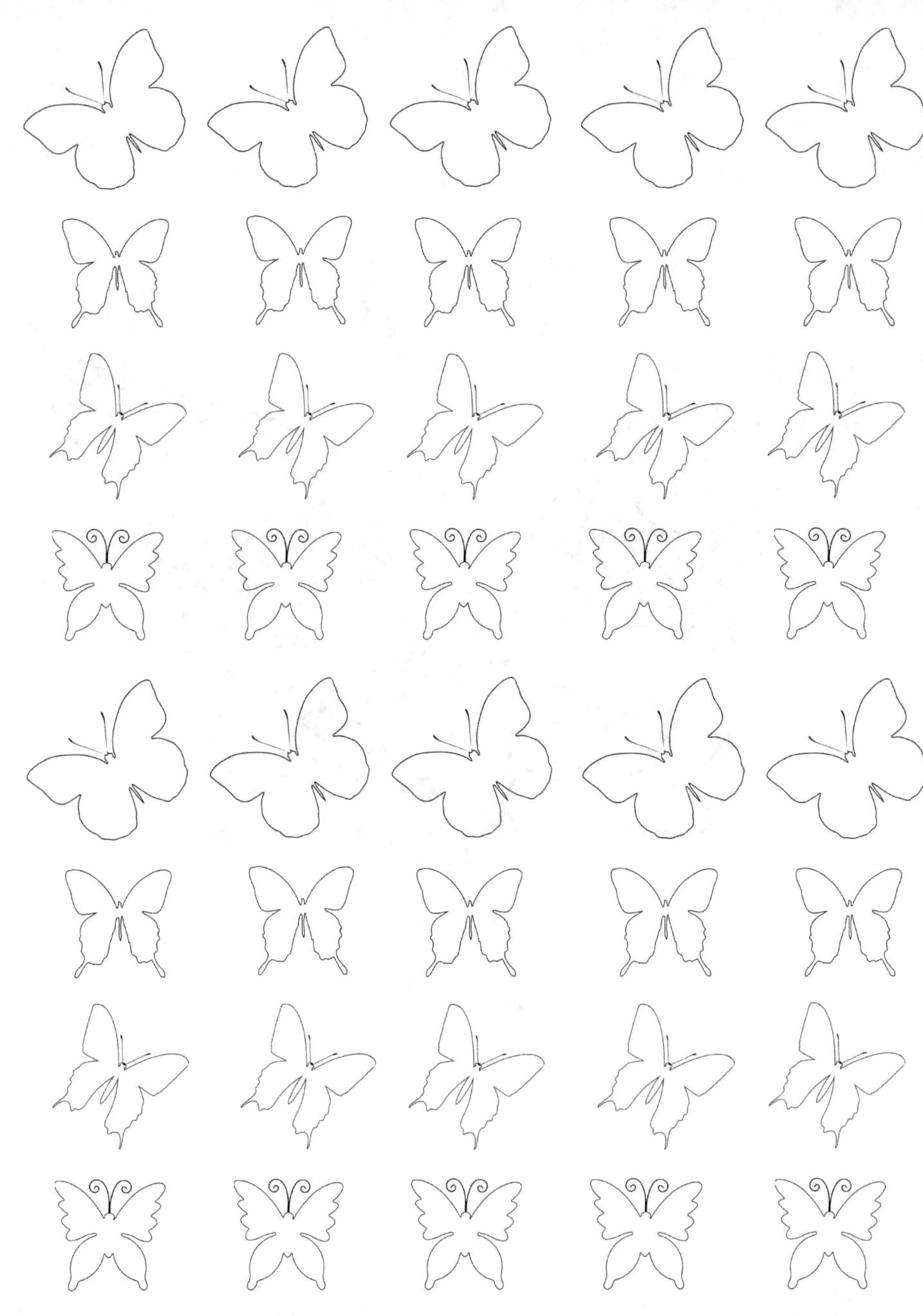

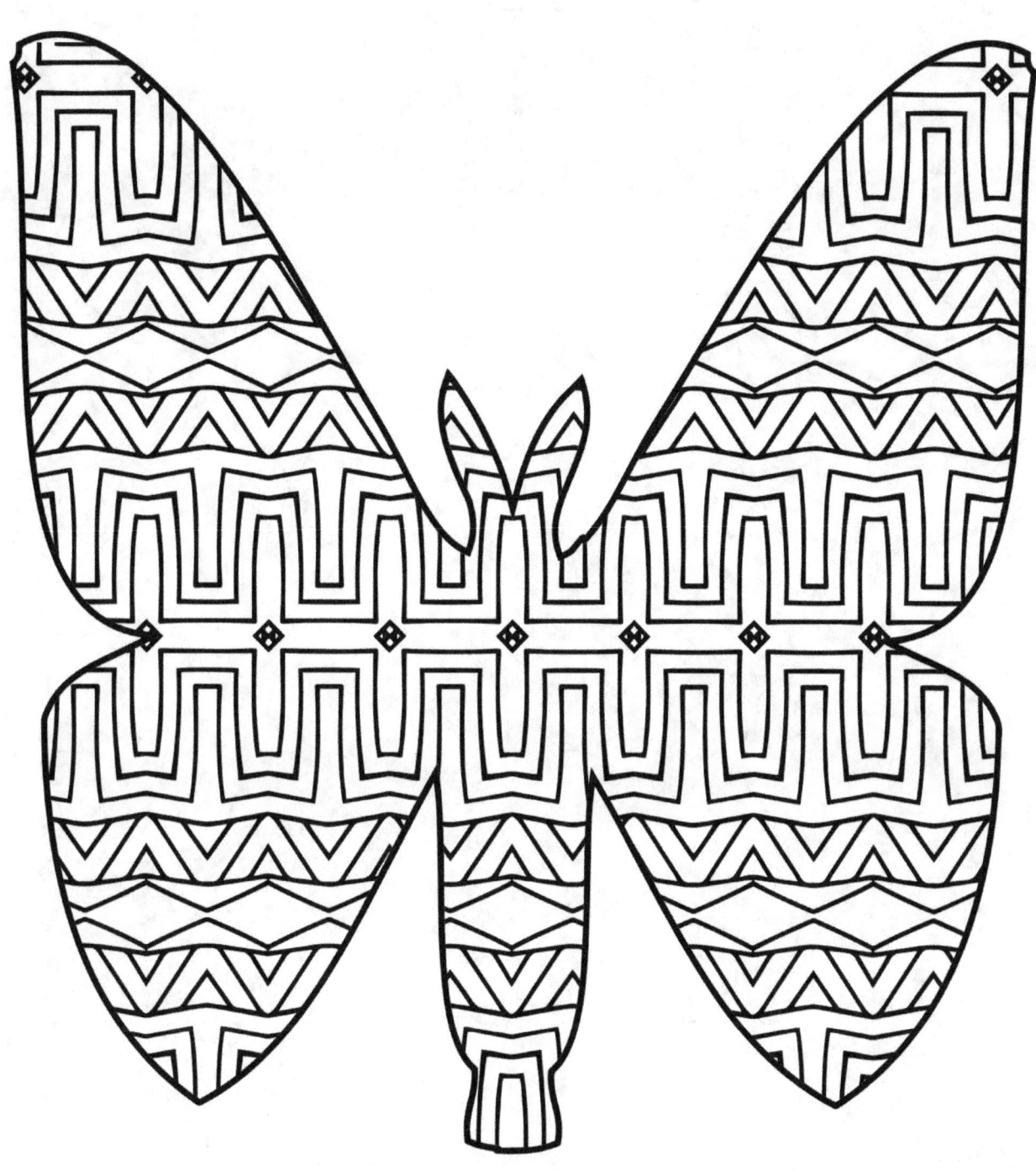

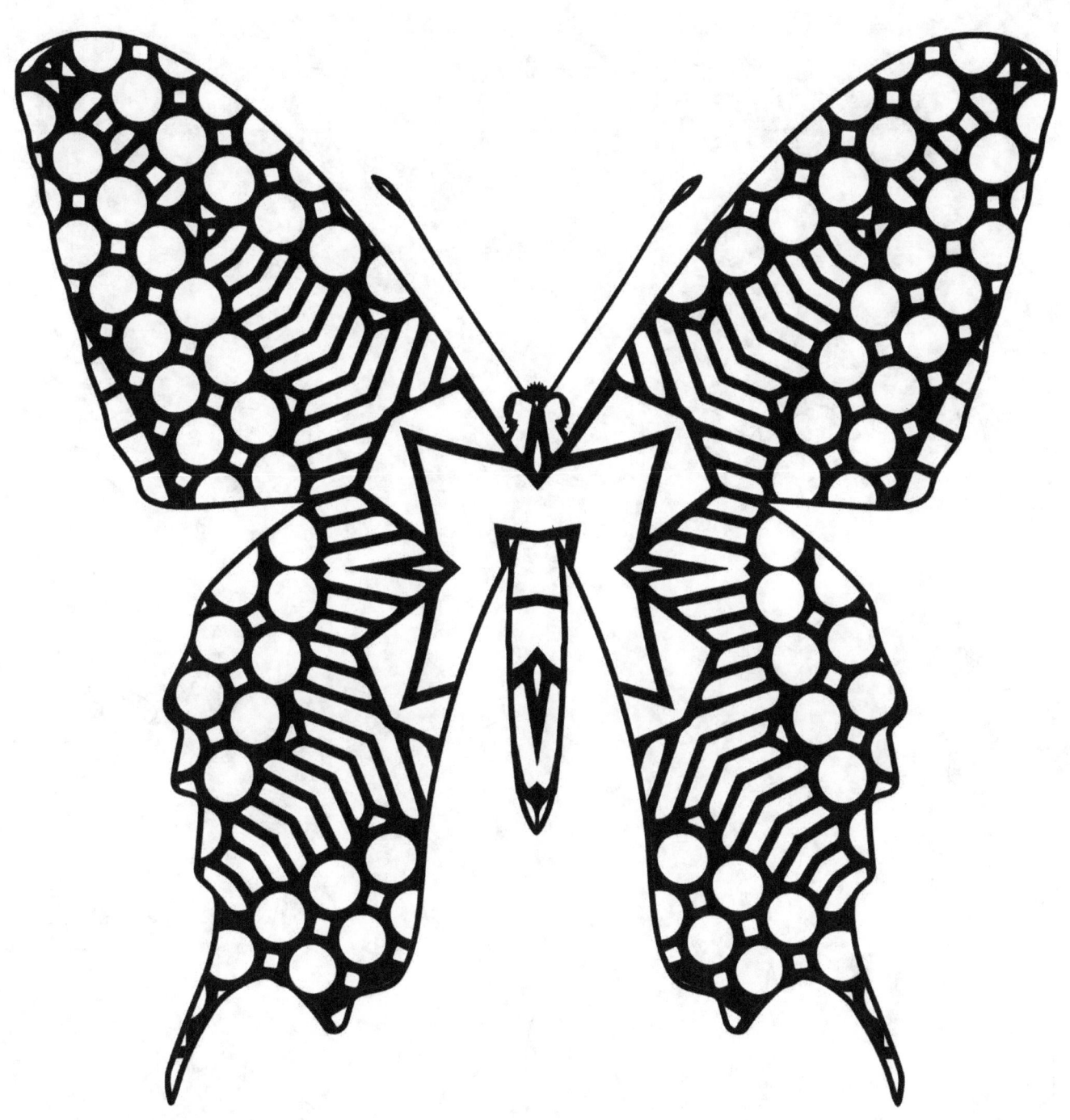

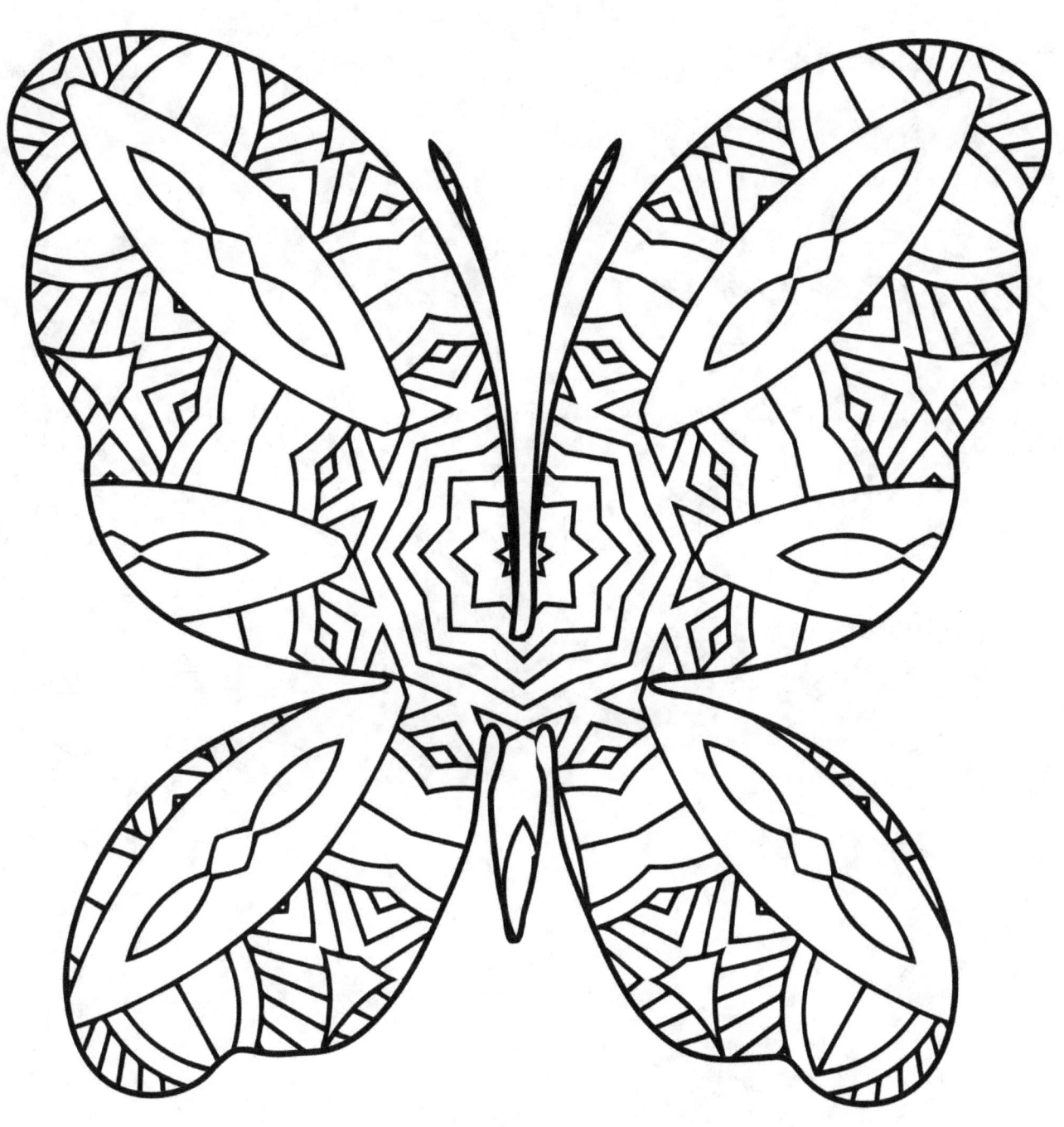

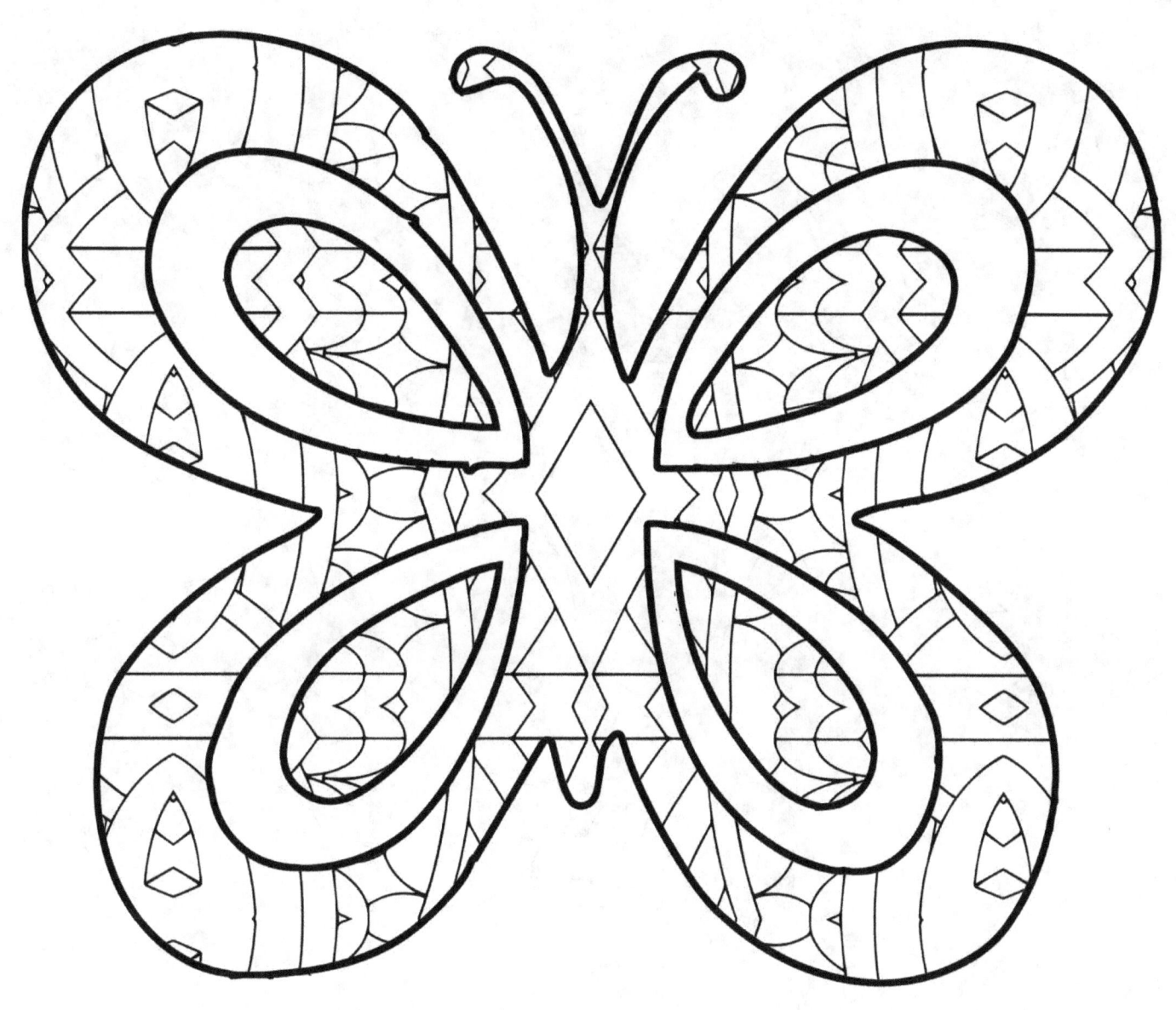

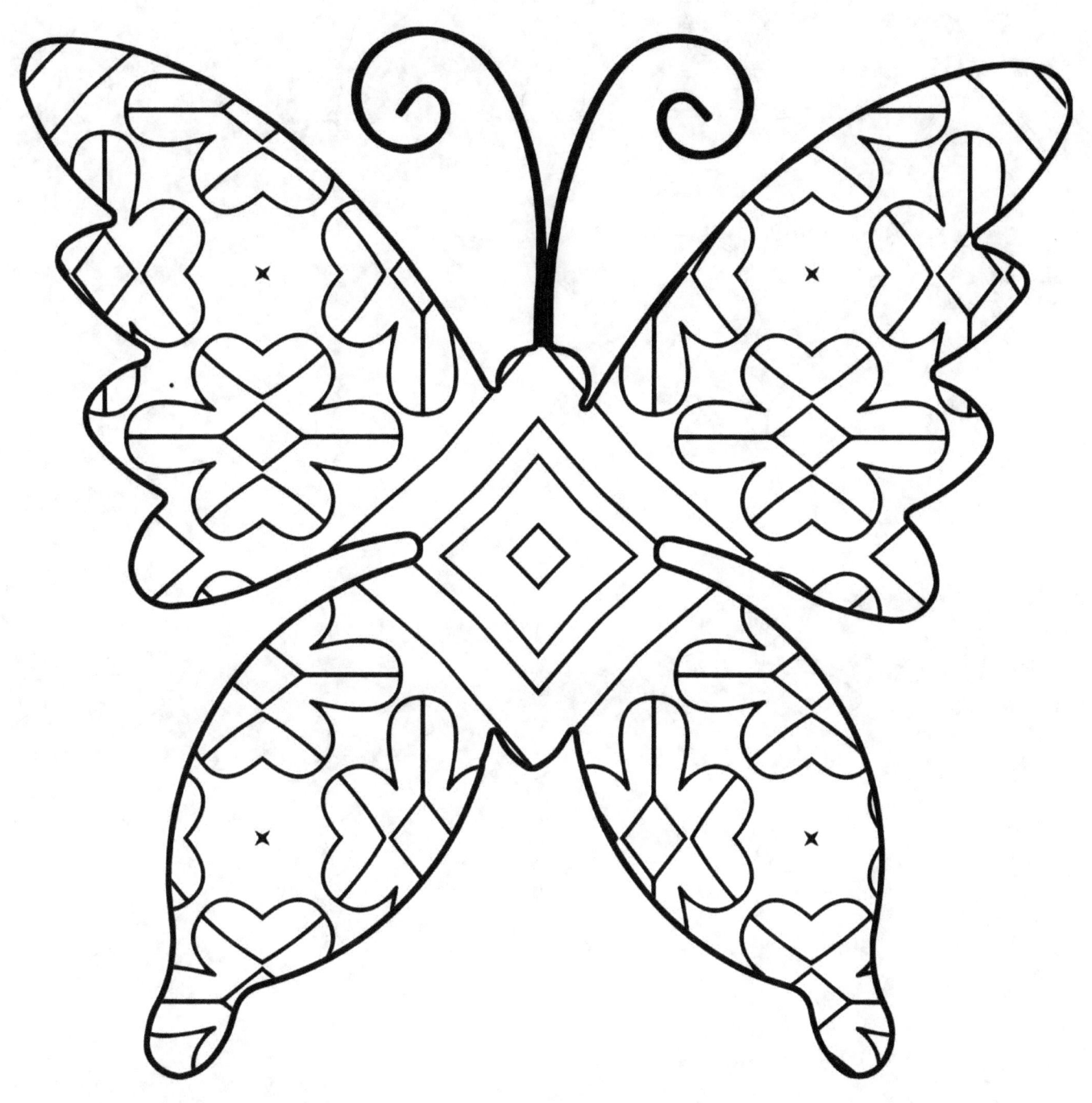

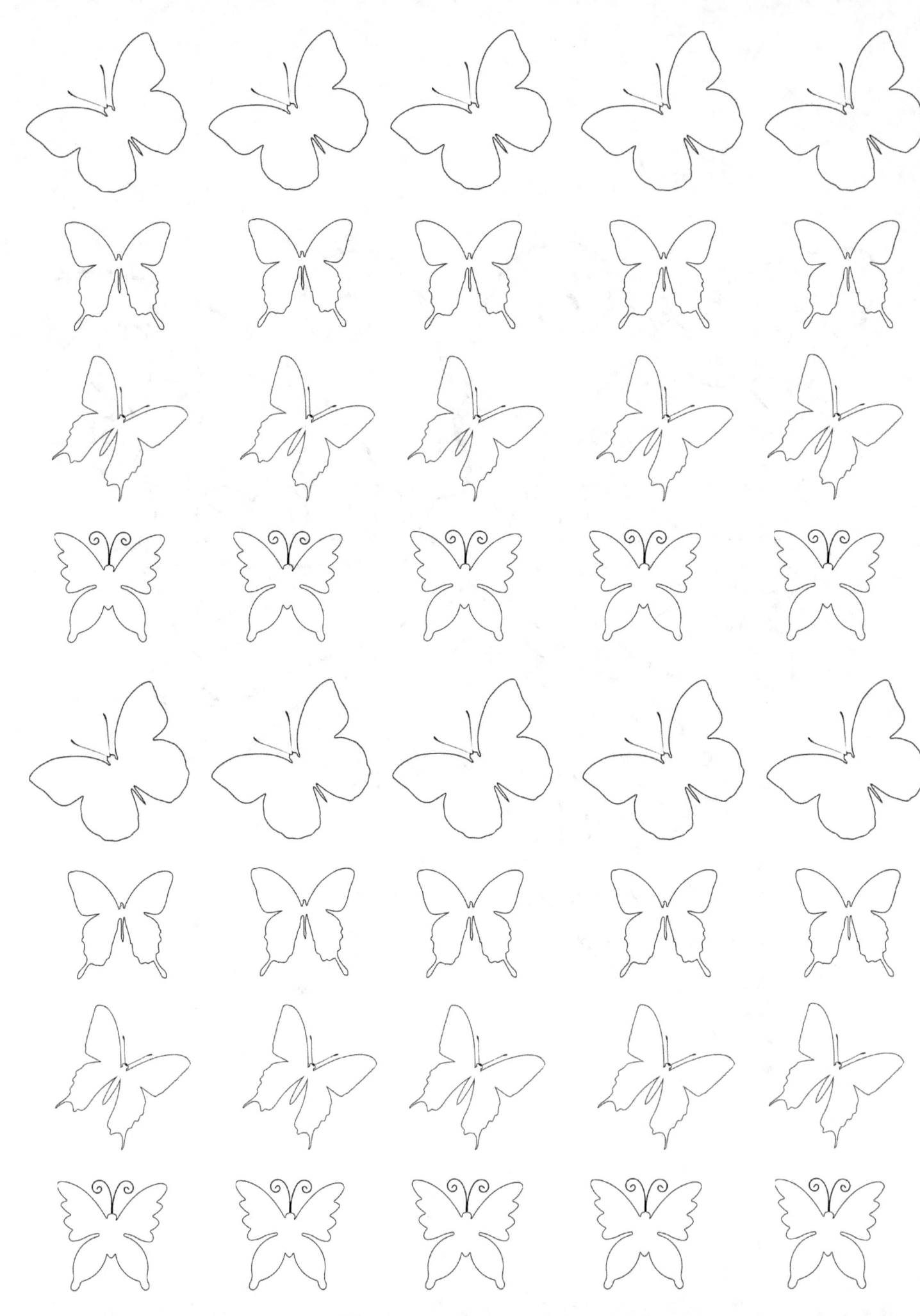

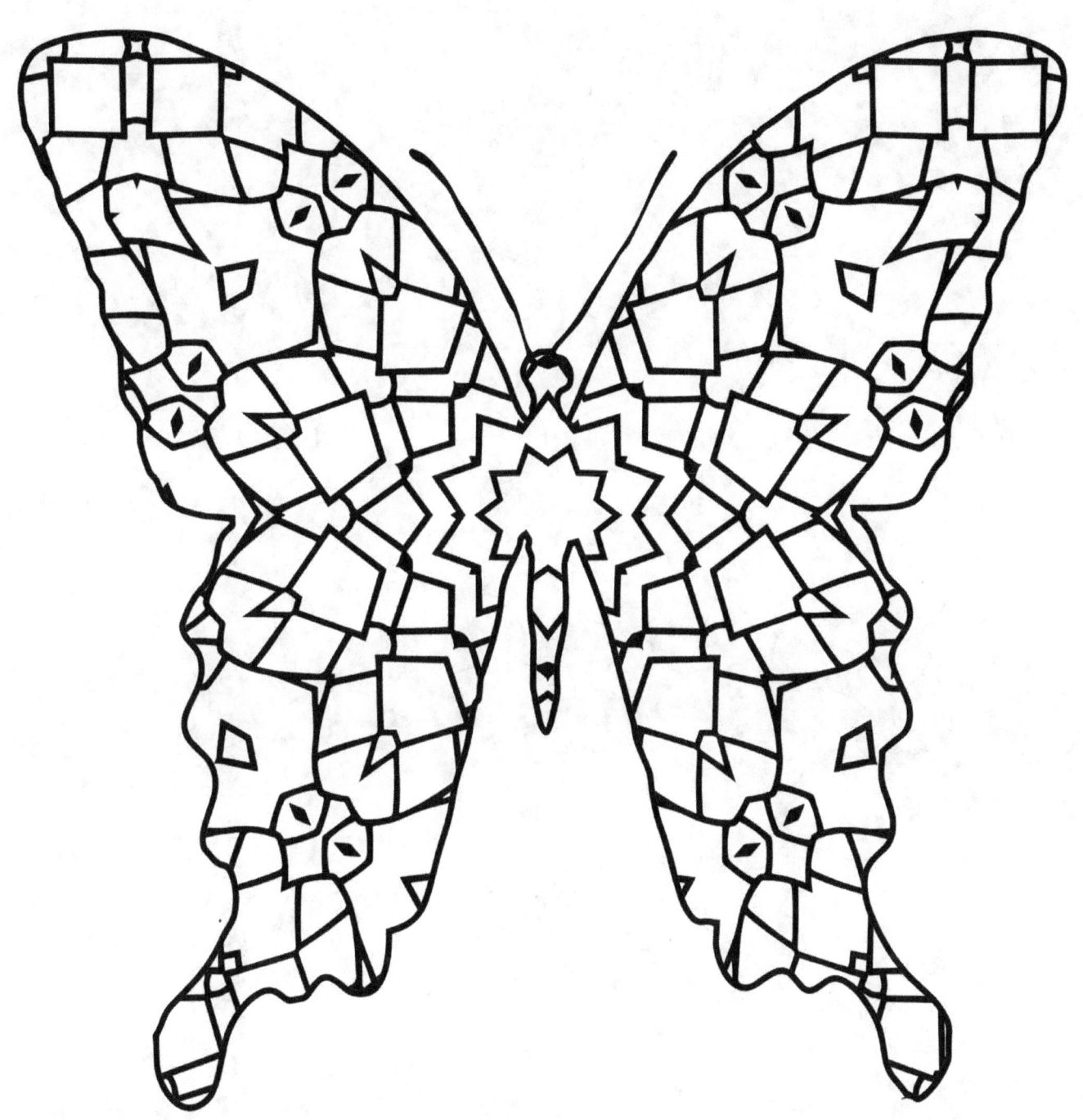

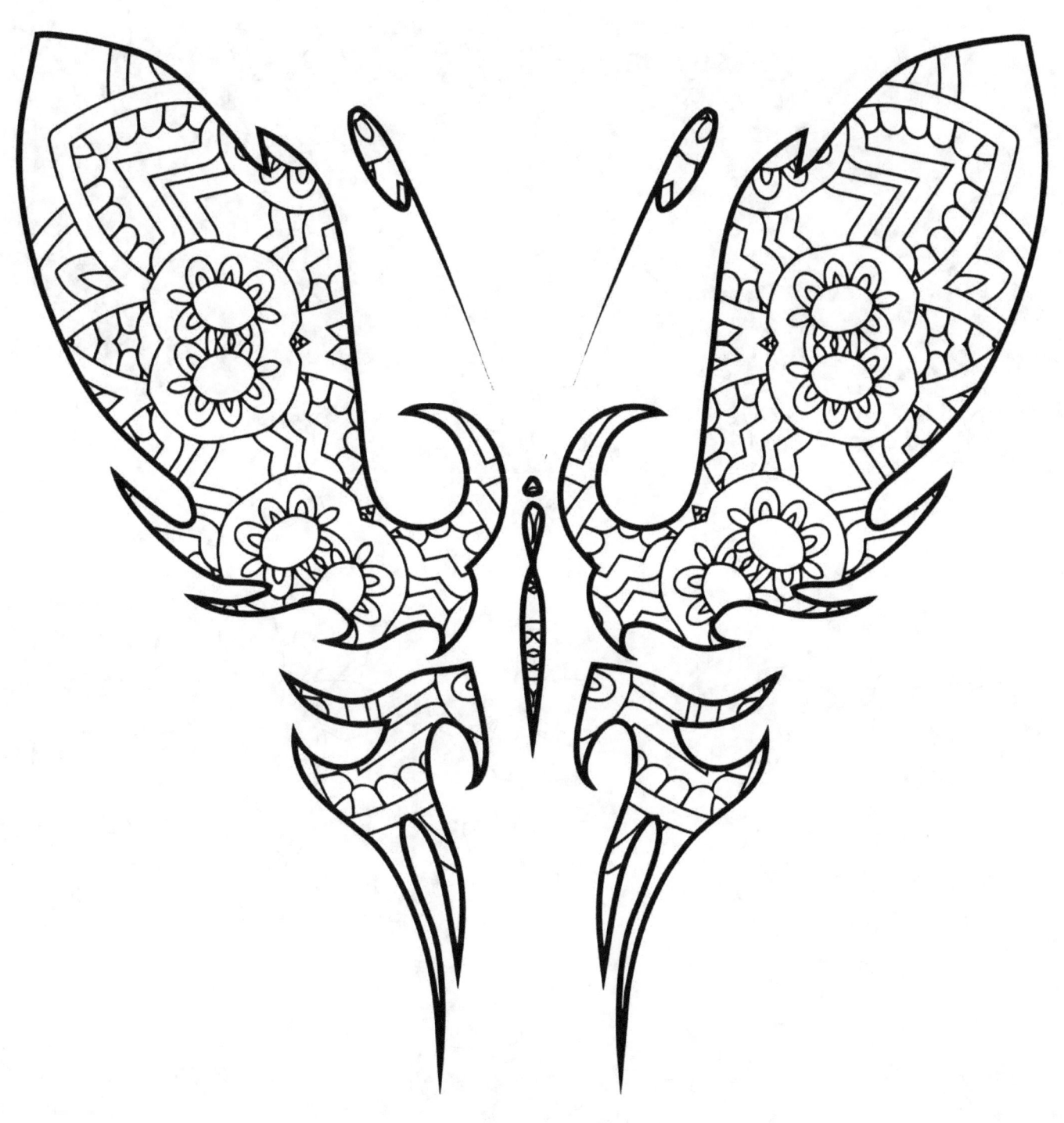

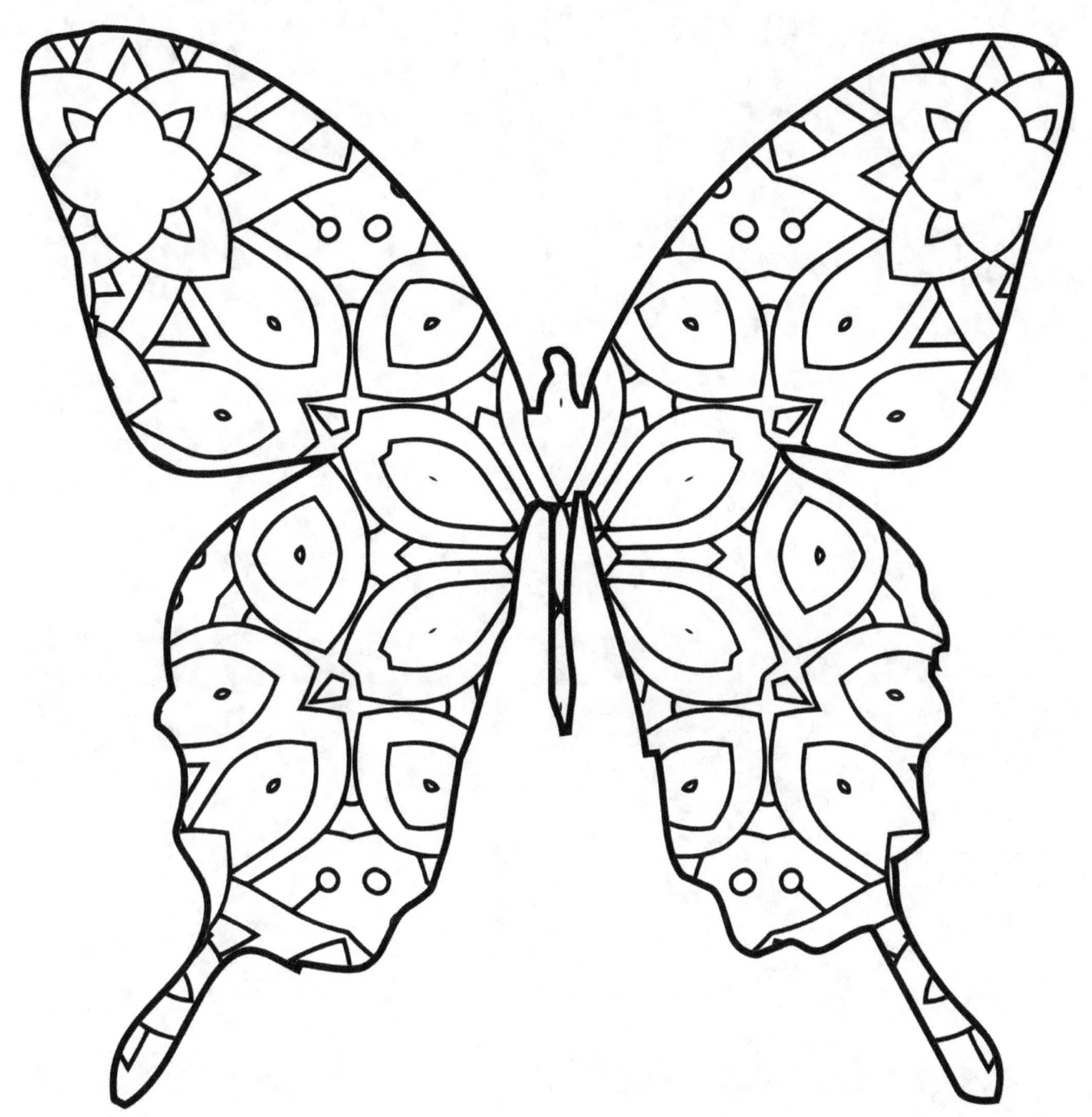

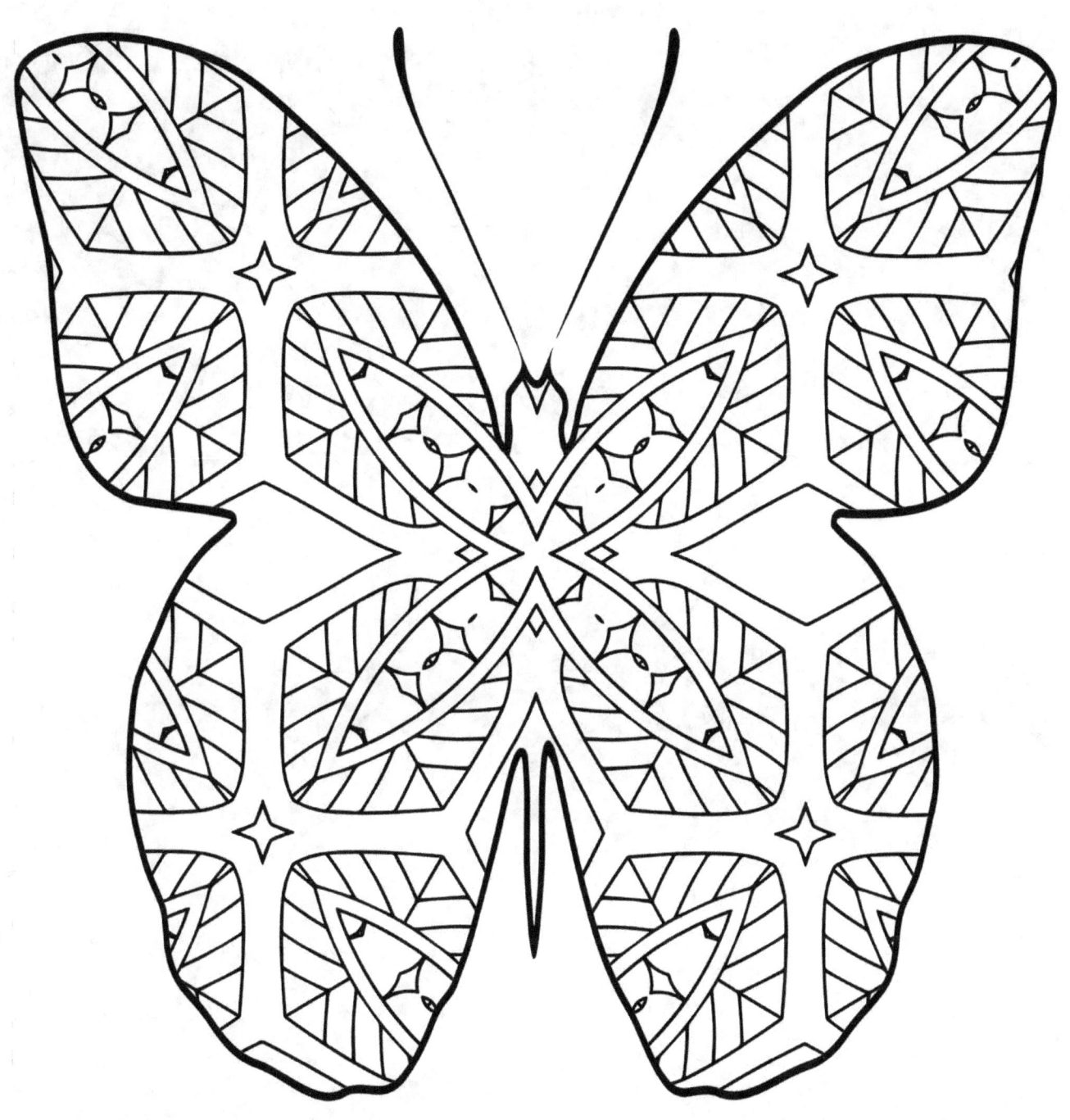

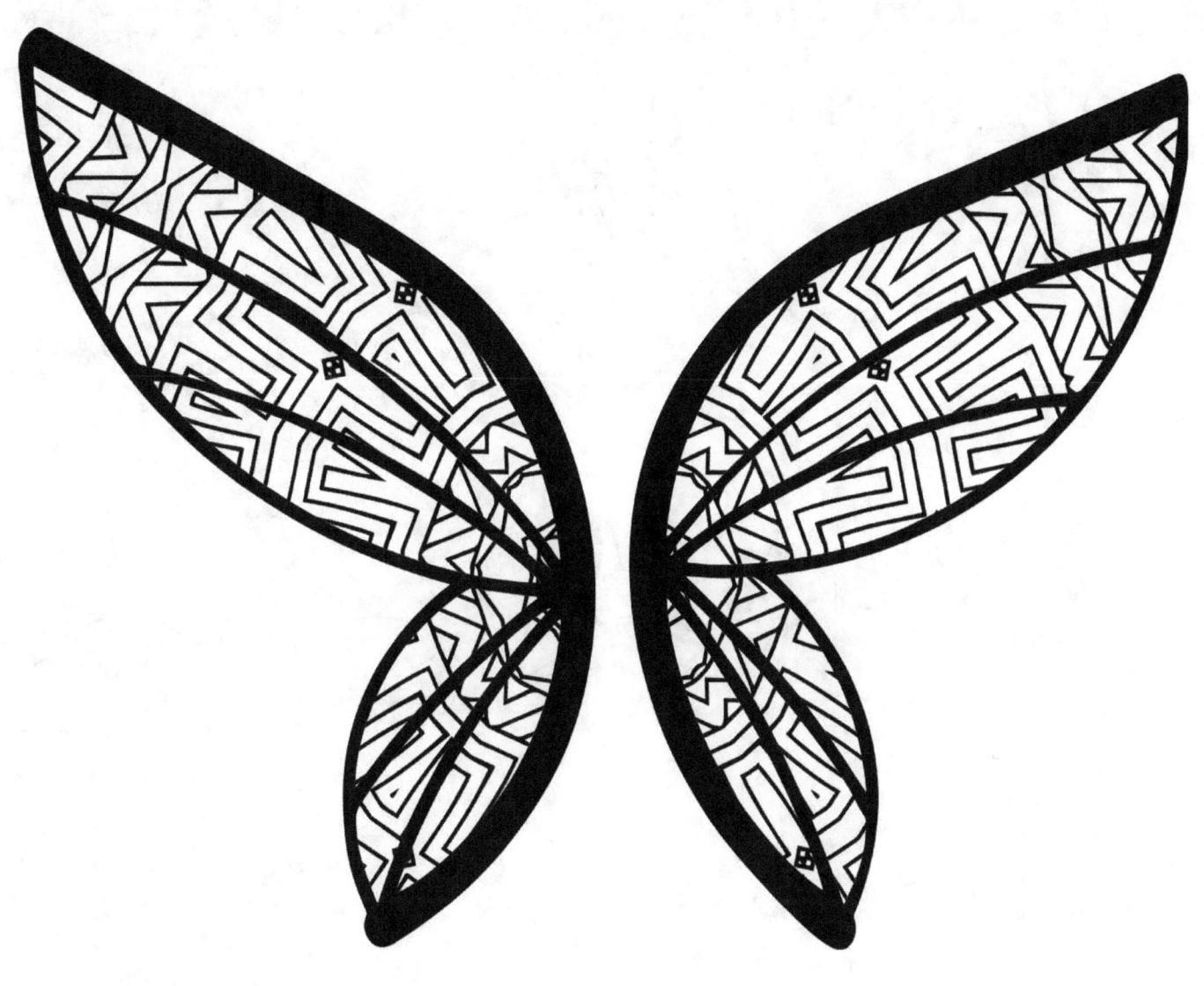

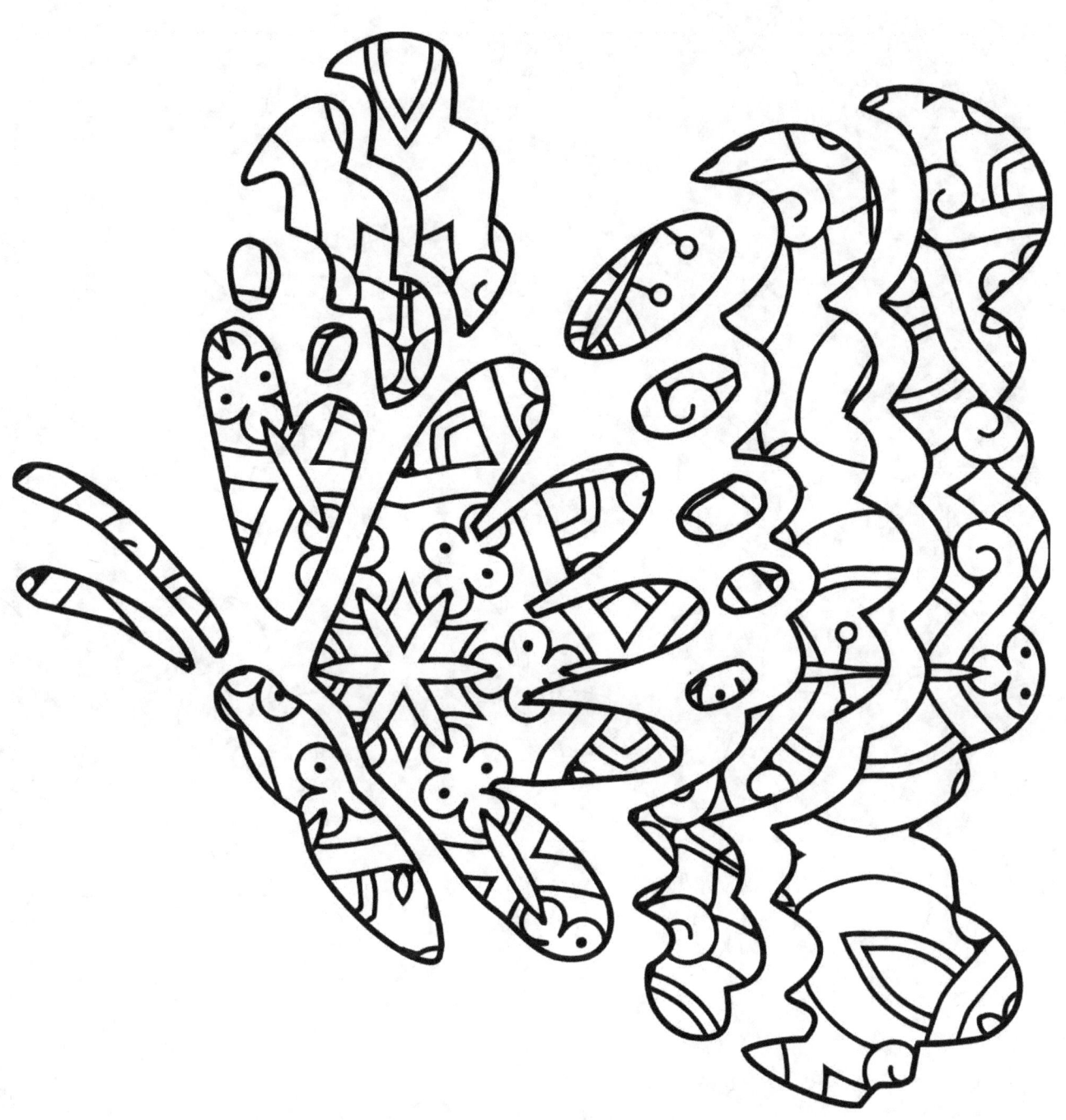

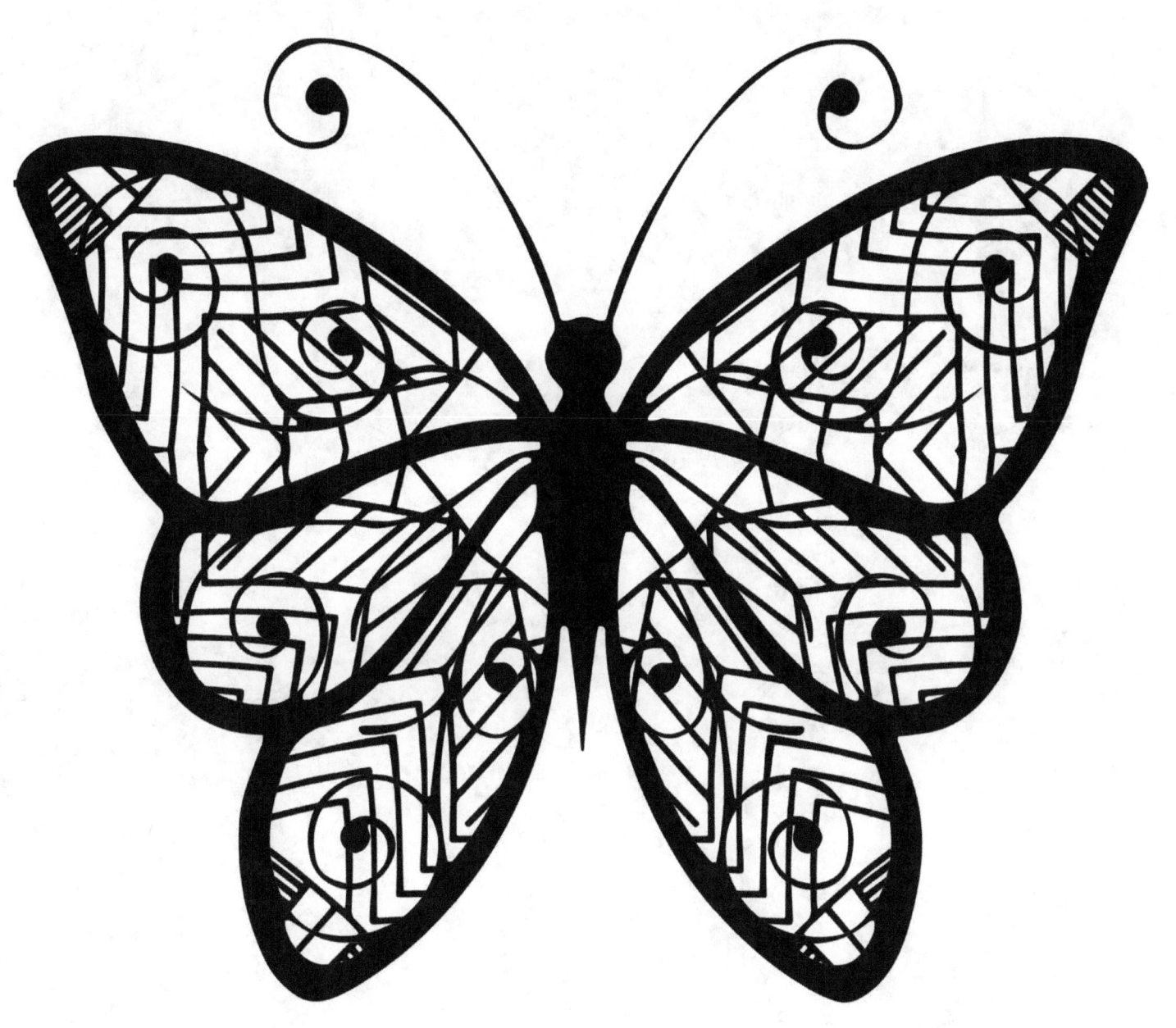

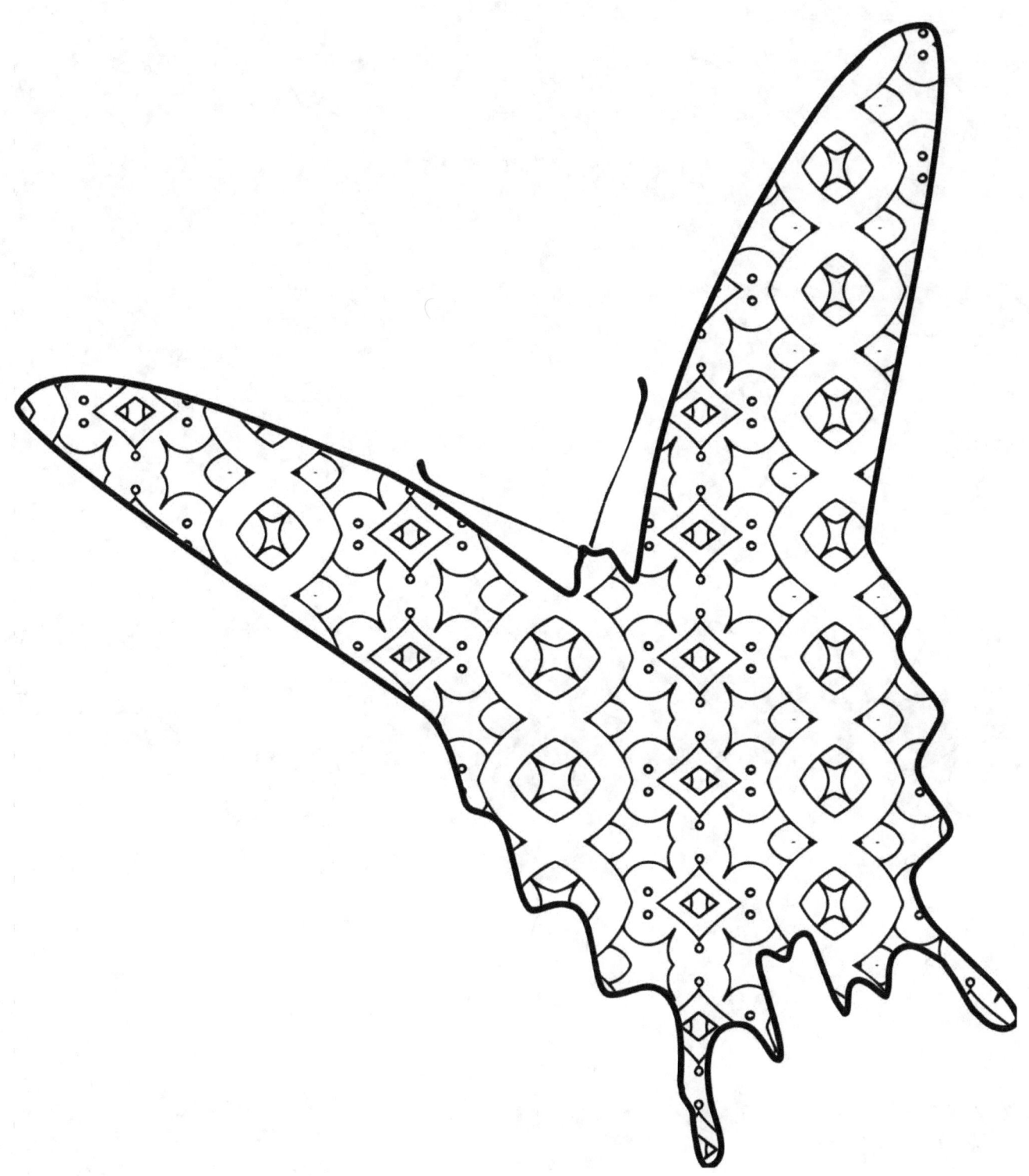